What you feed

your dog

affects the quality

and the q-u-a-n-t-i-t-y

of your dog's life

FIRST EDITION

FEEDING YOUR DOG FOR WELLNESS & LONG LIFE

1995 by Gerald A. Strutz, PhD.

Library of Congress Catalog Number 95-094688

ISBN: 0-9648011-0-8

Published by 'A Light at the End of the Tunnel Books
4711 East 128th Street East, Tacoma, Washington 98446-4909
Printed in the United States of America

FORWARD

THIS IS A BOOK for the dog guardian. You will notice that I said *guardian...not owner.* We humans can *own* houses, cars, furniture, clothing...and alot of things...but not flesh and blood, living things. We are guardians to our pets...not *owners.*

THIS IS A BOOK for people who *love their dogs...* not for those who want a cheap means of security...or a living creature to *master.*

THIS IS A BOOK for *wellness-conscious people,* who know that staying well requires knowledge, effort, and persistence.

THIS IS A BOOK for *longevity-conscious people,* who enjoy life...want to live as a well person for as long as possible...and want their pets to enjoy the same advantages they do.

THIS IS A BOOK for those people who know that *"you are what you eat,"*...that nutrition is of primary importance to wellness and longevity...and want their pets to benefit from this awareness.

THIS IS A BOOK for *Golden Rulers*...those people who unselfishly *want the best for others,* including their dogs.

THIS IS A BOOK for people who *consider their dogs their companions and best friends.*

THIS IS A BOOK *for your dog.* You'll see that your dog is very much like you...but, of course, he does not read. *So you'll have to read this book to him.*

I WROTE THIS BOOK for the dog guardian who fits all of the descriptions on the page to your left. I tried to keep from getting too technical and wordy.

But my primary concern was to teach you...teach you the great importance of nutrition for your dog...and for you too.

I WROTE THIS BOOK because I wanted to teach you how to select the best foods for your canine companion; how to keep him well; how to help him to live a long, enjoyable life.

I WROTE THIS BOOK because I wanted to make you aware of the great number of dangers in many of the foods dogs are fed.

I WROTE THIS BOOK because I wanted to warn you of the many toxins to which your dog may be exposed.

I WROTE THIS BOOK because I know that a dog who is nutritionally sound will not have the stress of fleas and pests, neither internally nor externally. And this is not only stressful to your pet, but to you too... not to mention the costs involved.

I WROTE THIS BOOK because a nutritionally sound dog will not have the skin problems many dogs have.

I WROTE THIS BOOK because the pet guardian is subjected to a constant barrage of potentially harmful and dangerous advertising in the media.

I WROTE THIS BOOK to show you that your dog is not really very different from you in his nutritional needs...nor his other needs either.

I WROTE THIS BOOK because I love animals.

I WROTE THIS BOOK for your dog.

I WROTE THIS BOOK for you.

ACKNOWLEDGMENTS

Acknowledging credit to all of those who have made a contribution to the writing of a book is indeed an impossibility...as anyone who has ever done so knows. So in making these acknowledgments, let me say that there are hundreds of people and pets who will not be mentioned in this single page of thanks.

The number-one person to whom I gratefully acknowledge thanks is my wife Anne, who has been involved with pets her entire life...and has worked in the pet field throughout her teen and adult life.

I also owe the pet industry a debt of gratitude, because it was working with pets that brought us together initially. And it has been this involvement with pets that has been a large part of our lives.

Dozens and dozens of veterinarians...both excellent and not so excellent, have helped to provide me with a challenge and purpose for becoming involved vocationally with dogs.

My parents, and my older brother Bob passed-on their love of dogs to me, for which I am grateful.

Fellow-writers of books on dogs have provided me with greater interest for reading and research, stimulating my desire to know more.

Max and Marci, two handsome chocolate Standard Poodles, now in their 13th and 8th years, have been an added inspiration to me...as were Buster; Duke; Ginger; Peppy; and Sonny-Boy. THANKS.

TABLE OF CONTENTS

Chapter 1   page   1 - 7
Wellness & Longevity for Humans & Canines

Chapter 2   page   8 - 20
What Your Dog Should Not Eat

Chapter 3   page   21 - 27
Your Dog's Food Needs to be Balanced

Chapter 4   page   28 - 36
Protein to Help Your Dog Grow

Chapter 5   page   37 - 41
Carbohydrates: Brainfood for Your Dog

Chapter 6   page   42 - 47
Fat: The Good & The Bad

Chapter 7   page   48 - 59
What Vitamins Does Your Best Friend Need?

Chapter 8   page   60 - 66
But Don't Forget the Minerals

Chapter 9   page   67 - 73
Food Allergies: Misery & Death

Chapter 10   page   74 - 83
Alternative Nutritional Therapies

Chapter 11   page   84 - 90
A Recipe for Wellness & Longevity

C H A R T S

Chart 1 Canine-Human Ages   page   5
Chart 2 Daily Caloric Needs   page   24
Chart 3 Protein Requirements   page   36
Chart 4 Carbohydrate Requirements page   41
Chart 5 Fat Requirements   page   46

CHAPTER 1

WELLNESS & LONGEVITY FOR HUMANS & CANINES

At one time in our history we believed that the physiological, psychological, and sociological needs of canine and human beings were worlds apart. We thought that the dog was a dumb animal, and presumed that they were very unlike us. Some people still think of the dog as a wild animal...wolf-like...with a proclivity for fighting...and requiring a diet of raw meat. But in the last two decades we have learned that these beliefs are unfounded.

OF COURSE, WE ONCE THOUGHT THAT THE WORLD WAS FLAT TOO.

Both man and canine have the ability to learn. And we have now learned that the canine and human are very similar in all of their health needs: adequate and proper physical exercise; a balanced, planned nutrition; effective hygienic care; controlled stress; and physical touch and social communication between canines and humans. And as we learn more about canine development, we see more and more similarities between the dog and the human being. Obviously, there are *differences* between the canine and human species, but definitely fewer than was once thought. Some of these major differences are listed:

the dog moves on all-fours...as we once did;

the shape of the jaw and teeth; but what about the caveman's mandible and chompers?

a vocal-cord sound difference; humans can make the sound of a dog, but making a human sound is more difficult for a dog...

the smaller brain of the canine; the caveman comparison again. Total cognitive abilities are lower with the canine, particularly in the 'reasoning' area

the manner of 'drinking' water; *(the dog laps water with his tongue while we humans pour the liquid down our throats, and some animals, such as horses and cows suck the water up)*. If we humans had to drink out of a bowl on the floor, we'd drink differently too.

the canine paw is much more inefficient than the human's hand and fingers. Try doing anything without the use of your hands, and see. You would be eating out of a bowl too.

digestive; mouth digestion, mastication, regurgitation. *(See Chapter 5 for more detail)*

the greater hirsutity of the canine body adds problems with hygiene, skincare, and external parasites). Check out the Neandrathal man again.

canines can manufacture their own vitamins C and D in their bodies, while humans cannot...though we're not sure just how much. Perhaps humans could do this at one time as well.

the normal temperature of the dog is 101.5, while humans have a 98.6 normal temperature. lifespans are at a different rate, and the length of longevity is also dissimilar, as will be detailed below.

There are other technical and minor differences. These examples of dissemblance have caused the canine species to lag far behind the human in the ability to learn and progress. But we now have learned that there are **more similarities than there are dissimilarities.** And a pet guardian who is knowledgable will help to install a long and healthy life. That person can have a companion who is able to take part in a mutual sharing of life between canine and human being, and will be a trusted, loyal friend... regardless of these differences. We are learning that humans with extremely varied cultures and color can live together in harmony, but it takes learning, understanding, and effort. And with these same guidelines, the union between canine and human is getting closer as well.

The domesticated dog, by desire, is subservient to their human guardians. They recognize these differences and accept them. And they are happiest when they're able to do a service for their human companions. The human guardians need to encourage this bonding between the two species.

HUMAN & CANINE LONGEVITIES ARE DIFFERENT

The major bodily functions and needs of the human and the canine are basically the same. But when it comes to longevity the similarities cease. Humans outlive the canines 5-1 at this time. There are several reasons for this. One of the biggest reasons for this lower life expectancy for the canine is the dog's nutritional deficiencies, which is the main subject of this book. Stress plays a role too, as does the reduced physical exercise dogs experience as 'house-dogs' living in the city. Other reasons for the lower longevity of canines are: mistreatment of the canine by humans, lower incidence of health care, and a less-sanitary existence than that of human beings.

Six-hundred years ago humans only had a life-expectancy of about 30 years; Three-hundred years ago the average human could expect to live to 40; Two-hundred years ago, 50 years was the expectation of life; One-hundred years ago it was 60; and now, as we come to the end of the twentieth century, 75.

And, as we continue to learn how to provide our minds and

And, as we continue to learn how to provide our minds and bodies with more proper nutrients, it appears likely that we will continue a lifetime extension...perhaps to 120 by the end of the 21st century...and canines, who are limited to about 15 years now, may advance their average longevity to the age of 35 or 40 by then, if we humans afford our canine friends with optimal nutrition and care.

This great increase in life expectancy for humans has come about primarily by learning, resulting in a greatly improved human life style. An earlier lifestyle change for humans was in sanitation, particularly in purification, which began in the last half of the 19th century. Learning in the area of nutrition, assisted by greater availability of food, brought about by improved agricultural practices were significant in making this progress. Balanced diets, with the vitamins and minerals that are needed to build resistance against sickness and disease, came along next. And this same nutritional change is now beginning to take place for canines.

The canine species has a normal life expectancy of something under 15 years in the first half of the 1990s. A 20-year old dog, while not really common today, does occur. And some dogs have lived past this a score of years.

As we are now understanding our canine friends more, and offering vastly improved care and treatment, it is expected that most dogs will reach the quarter- century mark...and many will go beyond this.

Prognosticators have often used a 7 to 1 formula for equating the age of human lifetimes to the length of canine longevity. Of course, this is not a realistic assumption. This formula would have a one-year-old dog, past puberty-age, equal to a seven-year old human. Really... a seven-year old father?

Actually, humans and canines do not mature at the same ratio throughout life. For the first ten human-years the canine matures at about a 20-1 ratio, and decreases as the species age. **A 10-year old human is at about the same maturation level as a 6-month-old dog.** Dog & human years are compared in the chart below:

HUMAN YEARS	DOG YEARS	RATIO
10	6 months	20-1
25	3	10-1
45	7	5-1
50	8	
60	10	
70	12	
74	13	4-1
82	15	
94	18	
97	19	3-1
100	20	

CHART 1

According to the Guiness Book of Records, the oldest dog-age recorded is 27 years, 3 months. There are claims of many dogs living to be in the upper twenties. One claim is for as old as 34, though most of these are not substantiated by all authorities.

The same source, the Guiness Book of Records, records the oldest human living 113 years, 124 days, from Quebec, Canada; the oldest American, 112 years, 305 days...about 6 months younger.

As we continue to improve the nutrition of our canine

companions, reduce their stress, and give our pets better overall care, their lives will be more enjoyable, and their longevities will increase.

Total canine care is being advanced greatly now. The "outdoor dawg" is becoming a thing of the past, except for the uneducated guardians, who prefer to (or need to) think of themselves as "owners and masters."
We need to teach humans more about canine care. And perhaps this book will help to do this. Then more and more dogs will be reaching 20 years, 25 years, and even 30 years of life.

Your canine companion's quality and quantity of life is significantly affected by the same lifestyle criteria that is pertinent to your own wellness and longevity.... particularly in nutrition.

The cells of your dog's body must take-in oxygen, water, and the proper food in order to live. If any one of these is missing, he cannot live. The oxygen your dog breathes is carried into his body by his respiratory system. The breakdown of food by the digestive system provides the fuel for his energy. Oxygen transforms the food into fuel by oxidation. Without oxygen a dog could live only about five minutes.

Water is necessary to transport the fuel to the cells for body functions and the maintainence of life. About 60 percent of the dog's weight is water...90 percent of the blood. He could only live about 6 days without water.

Water regulates the dog's body temperature;
serves as a lubricant in the joints;
carries carbon dioxide to the lungs, and salts &
nitrogenous wastes to the kidneys for expulsion;
exists as a shock absorber in the eyes, spinal cord, and
amniotic sac during pregnancy;

acts as a solvent for all digestion products.

The first two needs, AIR & WATER, are relatively simple to obtain... though clean, uncontaminated air and water are becoming less available as technology increases in complexity. There are increasing problems getting clean air and water.

Ozone, the primary component of smog, is a gas formed when nitrogen oxide and hydrocarbons combine in sunlight. Gas-run vehicles are the chief sources of ozone, which spew out about 15 million tons of hydrocarbons and nitrogen oxides into the air daily. Utilities, oil, and chemical plants are also accounting for nearly half of the hydrocarbon emissions and half the nitrogen oxide emissions in the U.S. Dogs are just as susceptible to 'bad air' as humans. And plants are also victimized by 'dirty' air. As the number of humans and canines increase each decade, more trees are cut down; wetlands and prairies are invaded.

The Nature Conservancy says that "Extinctions are accelerating worldwide. Our planet is now losing up to three species per day...and increasing. 20% of all Earth's species could soon be lost..." Air and Water are necessary for life...for humans, animals, and plants.

After air and water, the third need for dogs is *proper nutrients*. Food consumption is the major objective of this book ...to provide the canine guardian with a knowledge of the nutritional needs of their dogs so that they may give their canine companions a lifestyle conducive to the same wellness and longevity that we humans can now enjoy.

Not only do we need to learn **WHAT** to feed our dogs, but.....**WHAT NOT**.....to feed them.

C H A P T E R   2

WHAT   YOUR   DOG   SHOULD   *NOT* EAT

Your pet's *quality* of life, as well as his *quantity* of life is significantly affected by both WHAT YOUR DOG EATS, and WHAT YOUR DOG DOES *NOT* EAT. The major objective of this book is to offer information to the pet guardian regarding pet nourishment and care which will allow the guardian's canine to enjoy a relatively disease-free life, and perhaps twenty years or more of wellness.

However, before we plunge into the world of nutrition... what your dog *should* eat... let us first examine what could be the greatest reason why pets do not often live a disease-free life to the fullest......WHAT YOUR PET SHOULD NOT EAT.

Perhaps because of poor information and a lack of knowledge, pet-guardians may unintentionally reduce wellness and the length of our pet's lives by providing food which is not only lacking in nutrition, but can deal potentially death-resulting disease. In this way we are contributing to a less than optimal health; and a shorter life for our canine companions.

Well, ***don't get alarmed---get armed***---armed with good information about your dog's nutritional needs and available foods. And keep your canine companion in wellness...for a healthy, l---o---n---g life.

IF YOU **STUDY** THIS BOOK, AND **FOLLOW** IT, YOU MAY DO THAT FOR YOUR LOVED ONE, AND ALSO FOR YOURSELF AS WELL.

COMMERCIAL PET FOOD---ECONOMICS TRIUMPHS OVER NUTRITIONAL NEEDS.

If you read the commercial dog food sacs, with all of the color and photo enticement, you may be ready to eat the stuff yourself. And if you watch and listen to the television commercials on dog food, you may think that your dog is the luckiest dog on earth, just to be able to have that *scrumptious* dog food to eat.

Is there a financial gain for what you are being told? You betcha...to the **tune of 5 billion dollars a year for the petfood companies.** And these companies spend 175 million dollars a year advertising their products. For that kind of "bucks" you can bet that your're going to get a 'real' sales pitch.

If you thought that the sale of pet food was small potatoes, well, you can see that it's not that small---and it 'ain't' potatoes. In our country, **we spend 4-times as much on pet food as baby food.** Pet food is the largest-selling dry-food sold in grocery stores---even bigger than coffee sales.

The ad-makers have gotten much more sophisticated in their advertising of pet food products. You see all kinds of trick photography (though you probably don't realize it). The use of the computer has revolutionized television advertisements. Most of the nutritional claims are misleading and meaningless. In other words, if you pay close attention and listen--really listen to the words, *they don't really say anything.* but it sure sounds good. You're ready to run out and buy the product. And that, of course, is the idea.

"ECONOMICS" is the big word concerning the

to be able to sell for a little less than the competitor. As companies find cheaper ingredients to put into their product, they do so. These companies are constantly *shortchanging the pet,* in order to put more change in the pockets of those involved in the production and sale of the pet food.

Price is always an important factor to the American public, no matter what the product. Most people find it necessary to keep their food costs down...and they want to feed their pets at as low-cost as they can. Of course, "any pet food has to be good ---otherwise they couldn't sell it--right?" WRONG!

Though some pet foods DO meet the minimum daily standards, many DO NOT. The cosmetic effect for the buyer is often more important to the manufacturer than the nutritional quality for the animal. If it looks good, and it's propagandized well, it sells. That's the bottom line. Poochie doesn't know the nutritional value of the ingredients. He only knows if it smells and tastes good---just like most humans. And there is even some question about whether or not dogs actually taste...or just smell.

LET THE BUYER BEWARE

In order to keep the manufacturing costs low, the ingredients of pet foods usually look more like a list of ingredients in a can of garbage (if you can understand the disguised wording). A professor of Animal Science at the University of Illinois, James Corbin, once listed some of these ingredients used in cheap canned goods. Dr. Corbin's list included: gristle; lungs; pig snouts; cheeks; udders; pig feet; hog liver (condemned); hair; and tails.

Of course, you don't see such things on the list of ingredients---at least in those words. What you may see is the word *byproducts,* such as beef byproducts or chicken byproducts. This can include: moldy, rancid or spoiled meats: tissues severely diseased: discards, fecal matter, feathers, beaks, feet: waste materials and parts leftover after the slaughtering of the poultry.

THERE'S PROTEIN--AND THERE'S PROTEIN

Meat meal often listed in the list of ingredients is ground up discards of the slaughterhouse, even containing diseased tissue and high levels of hormones and pesticides. These very things may have contributed to the death of the steer or hog.

When the manufacturers of pet food boast of the "high" protein content, these "byproducts" make up a good portion of this much-ballyhooed protein. They emphasize the word "protein." Well, *there's protein-- and there's protein.* You could feed your dog cockroaches, and he'd be getting protein.

You will also see later, where protein sometimes CANNOT BE assimilated by the dog. **Protein cannot be metabolized unless the mineral intake of the dog is balanced.**

The words in the list of ingredients may include *vegetable byproducts.* This can be, and often is, peanut shells, corn husks, and other such uselessness which provides bulk to the dog food.

Well, now that you know what one national radio-commentator calls "the rest of the story," we need to confront the question "Can dogs and cats really use this "stuff" in their digestive systems in order to provide the necessary nutrients to sustain health and vigor?" What is the effect of this *junk* on the pet?

Dr. P.F. McGargle, in the book "Dr. Pitcairn's Complete Guide to Natural Health for Dogs and Cats" says "Feeding such slaughterhouse wastes to pets increases their chances of getting cancer and other degenerative diseases."

11

A frequent tricky listing on the package of pet food uses the terminology *Guaranteed Analysis*. This is no guarantee that the contents are nourishing. Those veterinarians who are authorities on animal nutrition say that the extra protein and harsh ingredients place an overload on the kidneys, liver, intestines, and other food processing organs.

VETERINARY NUTRITIONISTS
SPEAK OUT

Dr. Alfred J. Plechner, in his book "Remedies for an Epidemic, says that *"The poor-quality excess protein over the long-run is a prescription for kidney disease."*

The 1966 graduate of the University of California Davis School of Veterinary Medicine, further states, *"The kidneys have to process and excrete the toxins and nitrogenous waste products from protein breakdown. But nature never designed canine or feline kidneys to handle the volume of impurities that comes their way. The result is fatigued, irritated, damaged, and deteriorated kidneys after several years of life. Scar tissue replaces healthy tissue and cannot perform the normal task of filtration. Waste products are retained in the body instead of being excreted. These poisons often collect in the skin tissue and cause shabby coats and itchy, dry, scaly skin, a situation that mimics an allergic dermatitis. Left untreated, the toxic buildup leads to vomiting, loss of appetite, uremic poisoning, and death."* See Chapter 9 for more on allergies.

Another leading veterinary nutritionist, Dr. Mark Morris, Jr. states that a high protein food is "not good for your dog." Further, the doctor says an "**all meat diet can kill him.**"

Dr. Wendell Belfield, in his book "How to Have a Healthier Dog" talks about a case in which a cheap high protein diet was fed to a terrier who died of complete kidney shutoff and uremic poisoning. Dr. Belfield says that he kept the two shriveled-up scar-tissued kidneys in formalin to show clients what can happen to pets fed an inferior diet.

Byproducts do enough harm, but there's still more destruction in most pet foods sold commercially. *Red die #40*, which is included to create a fresh, meaty appearance, along with *sodium nitrate*, have been linked to cancer and birth defects. Some countries, obviously more advanced in animal treatment that we are, ban these preservatives.

PRESERVATIVES AND COLORING--
ADDED VENOM

Of course, the color isn't there for the animal. We know that dogs are not able to see and perceive color as we are. It is believed that they only see shades of black and white. The color is there for you---the buyer. It's designed to make *you* think "Oh, that looks good! Poochy will really like this."

Preservatives such as *butylated hydroxanisole* (BHA), *butylated hydroxytoluene* (BHT), and *sodium metabisulite* have all been linked to disease. Some of the suspected maladies are: liver damage, fetal abnormalites, metabolic stress, increased cholesterol, cancer, brain damage, weakness, difficulty in swallowing, and loss of consciousness. However, in all fairness, recent tests have favored BHA and BHT.

TOO MUCH SALT IS BAD

Excessive salt in foods, including commercial dog food, can lead to dehydration, which depletes the animal's potassium. A major role of potassium is to maintain fluid, electrolyte balance and cell integrity. It also is critical to the heart beat. The dehydration leads to potassium loss from inside cells. Initially the dog will be alerted by thirst, and will correct the imbalance in sodium/potassium by drinking water.. But if the canine is unable to get water, the potassium loss from brain cells can cause him to be unaware of a need for water, and in time, death can occur.

Consumers Digest, in a 1979 article, written by Francis Scherican Goulardt, said *"There is mounting evidence that a lifetime of eating commercial pet foods can shorten your pet's life, make him fatter than he ought to be, and contribute to the development of such increasingly common disorders as glaucoma, heart disease, diabetes, lead poisoning, rickets, and serious vitamin-mineral deficiencies."*

This example of out-spoken honesty may have made some enemies among the pet food manufacturers and some veterinarians. Obviously, if this book helps, along with the several others written about a *lack of concern* regarding our pet's nutrition and health, then it has assisted in a worthy cause.

NO STRICT GOVERNMENT STANDARDS
FOR PET FOOD QUALITY

Here's a blockbuster. There are NO STRICT GOVERNMENT STANDARDS REGULATING THE QUALITY OF PET FOOD. That's right! As hard as it is to believe in this day and age of government regulation.

"But," you say "I use a pet food that my veterinarian recommends." Unfortunately, nutrition has not been a large part of the veterinary training program in our nation's veterinary schools. (Nor in our medical schools either.) Wellness is not the primary purpose of the medical community for either humans or animals. Curing illness with drugs or surgery is the main intention for the medical practice.

But some of the more conscientious veterinarians and physicians have taken it upon themselves to study nutrition further on their own. This is indeed a minority. But those vets who have studied pet-nutrition thoroughly have made who have studied pet-nutrition thoroughly have made discoveries in their own practices concerning food-related canine ailments Let me say again. These veterinarians are indeed a credit to their profession.

Something positive should be said about commercial pet foods before you think *all* of them are worthless. There are a small number of pet foods that are acceptable as supplementary foods for dogs. Few of the better ones, however, are sold in grocery stores---nor are they advertised heavily. Find a petshop whose owners are nutrition friendly.' Ask them what their nutritional training is. Or locate a pet nutritionalist.

READ THE LABELS

Read the labels closely. Stay away from preservatives, artificial colorings and byproducts of various kinds. Reading the labels on dog food however, will not tell you the whole story. Perhaps there is a reason for this. If you really want your dog's food to be nutritious and balanced, don't feed your dog mainly on commercial food. Use dog food only as a supplement to his fresh-food diet. But select one that is not harmful to your dog.

Before we talk about good food for your dog, let's include some other foods which may have some harmful effects on your canine. In saying this, we need to remember that all dogs, just as is true with humans, are not alike. Some can tolerate certain foods, while others cannot. What disagrees with Fido may not disagree with Poochie. You will need to watch your pet's reactions to foods, and eliminate those which appear to have detrimental effects. More on this later.

We are just beginning to come out of the dark- ages when it comes to knowledge of our dog's nutritional needs. We know now that dogs are more like humans than was previous thought.

that used in cooking--nor can many people. Veterinary nutritional experts believe that perhaps 80% of all dogs cannot tolerate cow's milk, no matter what their ages. It is poorly absorbed, and impairs their body's use of nutrients. Also, it stimulates excessive mucous production, and can lead to other problems such as diarrhea, weight gain, chronic fatigue, and allergic reactions. Gassy stomachs, vomiting, or loose stools may be experienced by many dogs after drinking milk. Store-bought milk with Vitamin D can also rob the body of magnesium. **Yogurt and cottage cheese are better calcium substitutes.**

Milk has been shown in research to also interfere with calcium absorption, the very mineral it is suppose to provide. Fatty acids in the whole cow's milk form insoluable soaps with calcium in the intestine, then pass out in a malodorous stool before the absorption of the calcium. Yogurt will help to provide the friendly bacteria needed in the intestines. It's a good idea to add a tablespoon of acidophilus too. There is also a whey product that can substitute.

A multitude of growing evidence indicates a number of reasons why milk should *not* be a part of the diet of canines or some humans. In addition to the allergic reactions brought out earlier, there are other health reasons for eliminating milk from the diet: The elevation of the cholesterol level, which is believed to have a part in arteriosclerosis; the enzyme xanthine oxidase contained in the milk fat, made lethal by the homogenization process; and the consumption of many antibiotic drug residues left in the milk, caused by *fast-production-conscious* dairy farmers.

Like the human body, the canine-counterpart manufactures its own cholesterol. Every cell contains it. A diet high in cholesterol adds an unnecessary amount to the body, and may be a factor in the development of arteriosclerosis.

The potential for heart disease in your pet may be increased when you give your dog milk. *Xanthine oxidase*, an enzyme in homogenized milk fat, is added to the cholesterol. Small fatty capsules called *liposomes*, relics from the homogenization process, protect and transport the enzyme through the canine's intestinal wall. Persorption of the liposomes into the circulation is enhanced by gastrointestinal upset. The xanthine oxidase enzyme depletes plasmologen tissue, eating it away like removing mortar from between cement blocks. This lesion eventually becomes hardened by mineral deposits and surrounded by cholesterol. The heart has to work harder as the arteries are narrowed, and a heart attack may be eminent. The health of the dog's entire body is impaired as circulation decreases, and a variety of diseases are potential.

Vitamin D, which is added to homogenized milk, increases the activity of the xanthine oxidase enzyme, thereby causing more harm than good.

Eliminating milk from your dog's diet should be the rule. But for older dogs who have had milk in their diets for some time, folicin (folic acid) may reverse this damage, if it is not too extensive. See more about this vitamin later. .

Another reason to remove milk from your dog's diet is the potential for drug absorption. Test results in 1988 and 1989 on drug residues in milk were published in December of 1989 by the Wall Street Journal. The front page story reported that drug residues were found in 20 percent and 38 percent of the milk samples in the two studies.

After the 1988 tests, the FDA prohibited dairy farmers from giving sulfamethazine to milk cows. This drug is known to cause cancer in animals.

Other drugs still in use, whether legal or illegal, are still found in milk.   Some of these drugs are:

*chloramphenicol	*penicillin
*nitrofurazone	*clorsulon
*thiabendozole	*streptomycin
*ivermectin	*tetracyclines
*sulfadioazine	*aminoglycosides
*sulfonamides	

These drugs can cause such illnesses and health problems as cancer, skin rashes, aplastic anemia, anaphylactic shock, and nervous disorders.

The obvious incentive for the use of these drugs by the dairy farmers is money. At one time, the dairy farmer could produce about 2,000 pounds of milk annually.   Today, according to the U.S. Department of Agriculture scientists, an average of about 14,000 pounds is produced per year. Some herds average 25,000 pounds per cow, and some individual cows produce as high as 50,000 pounds per year---25 times the old production.

Rich farmer, poor cows; poor consumer

The rich farmer is in reality, a well-organized corporate conglomerate.

It is not a good idea to feed dogs raw eggs. The egg white contains aviden, a protein that renders biotin, one of the needed B vitamins, useless to the body. This can help to cause skin problems. Cooking neutralizes the avidin.

Some dogs can be allergic to eggs, even if they are cooked. This is something you will have to determine about your dog later.

Tomatoes are fermentative for many pets. Dogs differ, however, in the way they react to various stimuli...just like us. Unless your dog shows a fondness and tolerance for them, avoid them.

WHO SAYS DOGS NEED MEAT?

Pork, especially bacon or sausage has too much salt and soluble fat for your dog. It is often said by many who haven't really done their homework, that dogs are natural carnivores (meat eaters). Bull-oney! These same people say that the dog is very much like his ancestor, the wolf. Same comment. The dog of today is no more like the wolf than a human is like the ape. Granted, the caveman may have been rather "apey", but we don't go around beating on our chests and grunting---well, unless you're a professional "wrassler" doing it for show.

Raw meat is not good for dogs. It can cause both diarrhea and constipation, and you run the risk of serving him parasites and bacteria in uncooked meat. Dogs do not necessarily need to eat alot of meat. They can do well with only a little of it. (Just as we humans can). An all-meat diet will likely cause mineral deficiency eventually. Hair loss and red irritated skin, particularly in the groin and under the legs are also symptoms of mineral deficiency. Kidney disease is a symptom which may develop with older dogs. The concentration of protein is too high. This can cause a chronic irritation of the intestines, with a dark, foul-smelling diarrhea..

Too much meat allows the body's total nitrogen equilibrium to lag behind, as an oversupply of protein accumulates.. Experimental animals who have been fed protein to excess have been known to increase the weight of the intestinal tissue, liver, and kidneys.

A metabolism-stimulating effect persists for many hours after a protein food is digested. A dog that is consuming meat excessively may have a nitrogen imbalance, be more susceptible to degenerative disease, and may require a protein-free diet for a given time in order to return to a normal nitrogen balance..

A small amount of meat in the diet does provide needed

19

B12, and as a complete protein helps balance the incomplete proteins. Some meat in the diet adds to the palatability of food as well. A small amount of lamb or beef liver cooked with rice is an excellent use.

Meat is badly balanced in phosphorus, calcium, and magnesium. The calcium-phosphorus intake should be 1.2 calcium to 1 phosphorus. Meat is usually about 1 to 20, and is also poor in vitamins A, D, and E. **Your canine companion is better off with *no meat at all* than *too much meat*.** Ideally, however, a *little* is better. In the chapter on minerals, we will discuss calcium and phosphorus in more detail.

Protein can be substituted for fat or carbohydrates, but the reverse is not possible. Protein foodstuffs are indispensable to living organisms, basic constituents of every living cell, whether it is muscle in a human, the epidermis of a vegetable, leaves of a tree, or the fur of animals.

It is then, impossible for the dog's body to grow and repair damage without an adequate supply of the right quality and quantity of protein.

CHAPTER 3

YOUR DOG'S FOOD NEEDS TO BE
B A L A N C E D

DOGS NEED BALANCED NUTRIENTS

Before we knew much about dogs or nutrition, pet *owners* used to just pour some dog food in a bowl once a day, and that took care of *feeding* the dog. Now, we pet *guardians* know that much more is required in providing the nutrient needs for our canine companions. But just what is a nutrient?

A nutrient is a *chemical substance* which does at least one of the following:

(1) supply heat and energy to the body.

(2) build and repair body tissue.

(3) regulate metabolic processes

In order for a dog to enjoy good health, look good, have the vitality needed, and to realize a long and complete life, he requires a well-planned diet that provides the proper *balanced* nutrients. He needs the right amount of calories to provide ample energy. There are six essential nutrients your dog needs:

carbohydrates (including fiber); fats; vitamins proteins; minerals; and water.

We will refer to four of these nutrients as *macro-nutrients*, and two as *micro-nutrients*. Water, carbohydrates, fat and protein are the four macro-nutrients of ingestion, which provide the dog's body with heat and cooling.

21

ingestion, which provide the dog's body with heat and cooling. The energy of his body is drained by the oxidation of the three organic nutrients: carbohydrates, fat, and protein. They contain carbon atoms. Protein is known more for promoting growth, maintenance and body repair.

Without fulfillment of this energy, needed in all body functions, your canine could not live. In fact, the elimination of ingestion of *any one* of the four macro-nutrients would render your pet's body lifeless. And, in addition to just consuming them, the food substances need to be provided in *certain ratios and combinations* in order to give your dog the nutritional values for feeling well.

Next to oxygen, your dog's greatest need is *water*. About 60 percent of his total body weight is water...the major macro-nutrient in his body. Same for you. Obese and older dogs have less water in their bodies. Puppy has about 70 percent body weight in water, which is about the same amount as on our planet. And just what does water do for your pete besides satisfy his thirst?

Water *cools* your pet's body;

regulates his body temperature;

serves as a joint *lubricant*;

transports nutrients to the cells;

participates in bodily *chemical reactions*;

carries carbon dioxide to the lungs to exhale;

acts as a *shock absorber* in the eyes, spinal cord, and amniotic sac during pregnancies.

is a *solvent* for all of the digestion products, holding them in solution, permitting them to pass through the intestinal tract absorbing walls, and into the blood stream;

carries salts and nitrogenous wastes to the kidneys.

And *gives structure* to your dog's body by assisting cells

The canine body is about 90 percent water, just as yours is. Water is present in all of the chemical changes which take place in the body cells, and is the medium of body fluids. This covers both secretions and excretions, including blood, lymph, digestive juices, bile, urine, feces, and perspiration. Water is also a lubricant, preventing friction between the moving parts of the body.

Your dog's blood is 90 percent water. His urine is 97 percent. For solid waste to be eliminated, sufficient water must be present in the bowel. If not, constipation takes place. Water is *present in all chemical changes* taking place in body cells, and is the medium for body fluids.

Dogs lose water in six different ways: urination; perspiration; exhaling; gastrointestinal secretions; and via maladies such as diarrhea, vomiting, hemorrhage, fever, burns, and aging.

Balancing the intake of water to the loss is important. You should have water available at all times to your dog. If he is unable to get the water his body needs, he goes into a dehydrated state. The loss of 10 percent of body fluids constitutes a serious problem. Such a condition could lead to fever, electrolyte imbalance, circulation failure, renal function deficiency, and even poor absorption of food.

Before going into detail on the other five macro and micro-nutrient needs, let us first consider caloric needs. Then a chapter will be included on each of the essential nutrients. The formula below will show the caloric needs according to the canine's weight.

Use the weight chart. If you're dog is skinny, add calories per pound. If fat, subtract calories.. Ex: If your dog needs to gain about five pounds, add five pounds to the *Dog's Weight* column, and use the appropriate

Calories-per-pound-per-day. Subtract from the weight column if your dog is too heavy.

You can expect a female dog to be a bit smaller than the male. If you're not sure if your dog is overweight or underweight, examine the ribs and flanks by gently pressing in these areas. The flank is located posterior to the last rib. If the flank does not depress, the dog is fat. You should also be able to feel the ribs.

Chart 1 considers adult canines up to 150 pounds of weight for an average dog. The amount of exercise your dog uses up daily is one measuring-stick. A dog living on a farm and running over several acres each day will use many more calories than a dog in the city apartment, getting very little exercise. The chart is a good starting point. You will want to experiment with a trial and error method to find the right formula for your dog.

DAILY CALORIC NEEDS
OF THE ADULT DOG

Pounds of Dog's Weight	Total Daily Calories	Pounds of Dog's Weight	Total Daily Calorie
5	250	50	1350
10	420	60	1500
15	570	70	1750
20	700	80	1920
25	825	100	2400
30	930	125	3000
40	1160	150	3600

CHART 2

Continue this caloric amount for a couple of weeks.

Weigh your dog again. Continue the feeding until optimal weight is achieved. Raise or lower the amount of calories until you reach the desired weight.

But don't try to reach an optimal weight through feeding alone. Other factors also influence the caloric needs of your canine companion, such as getting ample exercise. If your canine companion is too fat, be sure that he is getting plenty of exercise before altering his caloric intake. Get out and play ball with your dog often...or see that someone else does.

A high-strung dog also needs more food than one that is lethargic. The active dog uses up more energy than the docile dog, particularly carbohydrates and fats for energy.

Whether your dog is fat, skinny, or just right, the controlling factor is the balance of *taking in* calories, and *using-up* calories...*energy balance*. Just as it is with you...his guardian. If you take-in more calories than your use, you get fat.

Both too little or too much body fat present health risks. Being too fat can precipitate hypertension. It can also give rise to diabetes in a dog that is genetically susceptible. Atherosclerosis, arthritis, and gall bladder conditions are among other debilitating diseases that can also be brought out by obesity. Excess fat makes great demands on the body of a canine, requiring miles of extra capillaries for increased feeding. The work load of the heart can be expanded to the point of damaging it.

Too little fat also increases the risk of disease control for your dog. Being underweight, he runs the risk of not being able to fight a risk-disease. Starvation can actually be the cause of death in the case of a wasting disease such as cancer.

Dogs are exposed to cold weather more than humans are. For this reason they have more brown fat, an adipose tissue that specializes in generating heat. Packed with pigmented energy-burning enzymes, the characteristic brown color gives it it's name. Producing body heat is more of a priority in cold weather. Brown fat breaks the slow metabolic bonds, releasing the energy stored as heat. Hibernating animals have a great deal of brown fat activity that generates heat while they sleep. Human babies have more brown fat than adults. Situated around their shoulders and backs, it protects their small bodies from brief exposures to cold.

Fat may also be accumulated by stress. Dogs experience more stress than humans. Even while eating, stress often is present for the canine. If another animal is present, even another dog or a cat within the family, he guards his food from possible theft. This may be an inherited tendency from the days of the wild dog. This aroused state may be interpreted as hunger, which might explain why a dog sometimes appears still hungry after eating.

This stressful state may promote the accumulation of body fat, as the stress hormones aid the breakdown of the energy stores of glycogen and fat to glucose/fatty acid miscellany that can be used to fuel the muscular activity expected as a reaction to an adrenal discharge.

Another cause of obesity, a lack of energy balance, is the absence of emotional stimulation. Boredom is one such emotion. Many dogs get very little stimulation of attention from their guardians, even to the point of being ignored. There seems to be nothing for the pet to do but eat or sleep. Such a lack of physical exercise is very conducive to overeating.

Age is a determining factor in setting-up your dog's diet. The caloric needs of a puppy are very different from an adult dog. A puppy needs more food-per-pound of body-weight in the first 12 weeks of his life than at any other time of his life.

Your 7-11 week-old puppy needs two and one-half times the nutrient needs of the adult dog. Example: while a 5-pound adult dog may need 250 calories daily, a 5-pound, 8-week-old-pup requires 750 calories daily.

The 12-25-week-old puppy is still growing, but his accelerated nutritional needs drop a little, to just double the adult needs at the same weight. So the 5-pound, 16-week-old pup needs 500 calories daily.

When your dog is six months old, drop to one-and-a-half times adult dog needs at the same weight. The 24-week-old 5-pound youngster would need 375 calories per day. Continue this ratio until your dog is nine-months-old, then slowly come down to adult maintenance calories.

Your canine companion may still continue to grow some until about 18 months, so if he seems to need a little more food than the adult dog needs, which are shown on the chart, add a little more---but only if he seems to need it.

The adult canine major nutrient requirements:

20% Protein-----50% Carbohydrates-----30% Fats.

Ex: 930 calories consumed daily by a 30-pound dog:

Protein 186; Carbohydrates 465; Fats 279.

Your canine companion may still continue to grow a little, until about 18 months, so if he seems to need a little more than the adult dog needs shown on the chart, add a little more, but only if he needs it.

Mathematically determined, 1000 calories consumed each day by the adult canine, purports to be:

09.0	grams of protein	(20%)
22.5	grams of carbohydrate	(50%)
13.5	grams of fats	(30%)

CHAPTER 4

P R O T E I N

TO HELP YOUR DOG GROW

Since protein is a basic constituent of every living cell, it is obviously crucially important to your dog's diet...as well as to your own. Protein is essential for the canine's normal growth and repair, and is the second-most substance in the body, next to water. All proteins are not the same, even though they are manufactured from the same amino acids.

A brief lesson on the functioning of protein within the body may be helpful for a more complete understanding.

The *atom is the simplest chemical substance known.* Two atoms may combine into a *molecule,* such as sodium and chlorine, which make common table salt. As the number of atoms in the molecule increase, the molecule becomes greater in size. Complex combinations of a large number of atoms, which are usually built around the carbon atom, are called organic compounds.

These organic compounds, which are called *colloids,* compose the plant or animal body. When these highly complex units contain nitrogen, they are termed *protein colloids. Both animal bodies and plants are made-up of protein colloids.*

The scenario is this: The plant digs its roots down into the damp soil, absorbing inorganic mineral elements. These elements are transformed by sunlight energy into organic colloidal substances. So when a steer comes along and eats the plant, his digestive system converts the plant protein into muscle. A natural food of human and canine is the plant or the animal which ate the plant. And, of course, the bodies of these species cannot grow, develop or repair damage without an ample amount of the proper protein.

The cells of the dog's body are formed from proteins. They may be the *calcium proteins* of the bones,

the *sodium proteins* of the liver,

the *potassium proteins* in the pancreas,

the *phosphorous protein*s in the brain/nerves,

the *iron and copper* proteins of the red blood,

the *sulphur proteins* of the connective tissues. Even the trace elements and the vitamins are proteins.

Protein is also partly responsible for replacing the worn-out cells. Nearly all of your dog's cells are constantly being replaced. Within each cell proteins are continually being made and broken down. Amino acids must be supplied constantly from food in order for this to take place.

Enzymes (catalysts that can change another substance without changing themselves), *hormone*s (chemical triggers that signal the enzymes to do what is needed for the body), and *antibodies* (large proteins in the blood that the immune system produces in response to the invasion of a germ or foreign body...germ-fighters) are each a part of the work of the proteins in canine and human bodies.

The balancing of electrolytes and acid-base are additional functions of the protein in the animal body.

In order to stay alive, a body cell must retain a constant measurement of fluid. Too much could cause a cell to rupture. Too little fluid could impair its functioning.

The primary function of the body, however, is energy.

And if fats and carbohydrates in the food eaten are insufficient, the protein will be used for that first.

You have probably determined by now, that **BALANCE IS A VERY IMPORTANT FUNCTION OF LIFE......BOTH YOUR DOGS AND YOURS.**

The canine and human obtain their protein from eating either animal or vegetable sources. Animal protein comes from dairy products, eggs and animal flesh. Vegetable protein comes from vegetables. All contain some protein. The greatest proportion come from peas and beans.

A misconception developed....... that the dog needs meat in order to maintain his strength and health.......that he cannot get this much needed protein from vegetables. We know now, of course, that this is untrue.

Herbivorous animals, such as the elephant, live on grass and leaves alone. And the huge, strong animal grows his great tusks from the calcium protein of the leaves. The elk lives on leaves, twigs and grass. The moose exists well on a diet of water plants and green leaves.

The canine body breaks down food proteins into their constituent amino acids during digestion and assimilation. Whether plant or animal in source, these amino acids are each useful to the dog's body as food, and he can stay well.

After birth, the canine lives on his mother's milk, which contains proteins, carbohydrates, fats, and all needed food elements. After being weaned, and during his growth period, the dog needs protein to grow. At this time, it is the most essential element in his diet. It must be supplied in adequate amounts. But, as he matures, protein becomes less and less important, and needs to be cut down as age increases.

Protein, called the building blocks of the body tissues, is broken down to simple molecules during digestion. These

30

simple molecules are called *amino acids.*

We are still learning more about these protein molecules. We believe that there may be as many as a million different proteins. Protein digestion begins in the stomach and continues digestion through the small intestine, with some of the amino acids reaching the liver through the veins of the small intestine. The liver builds up essential body proteins from the useful amino acids and eliminates the useless or harmful ones with the bile.

Proteins rich in available *iodine* must be accessible for a healthy thyroid gland. Iodine is a critical mineral in the hormone *thyroxin*, the hormone responsible for regulation of the basal metabolic rate. Though only a trace mineral, it appears in the canine body as the ion of iodide; More will be brought out about iodine in Chapter 8 on minerals.

Different from carbohydrate and fat, which are made-up of only carbon, hydrogen, and oxygen atoms, protein contains *nitrogen atoms.* Amino means nitrogen-containing, hence, the term *amino acids.* A protein is a strand of individual amino acids of 20 different kinds, with 9 being *essential,* 3 being *conditionally essential,* and 8 *non essential.*

An essential amino acid is one which the canine body cannot synthesize in the amounts sufficient to meet physiological needs. These indispensable trace minerals must come from food.

The essential amino acids are: histadine; isoleucine; leucine; lysine; methionine; phenylalanine; threonine; tryptophan; and valine.

The conditionally essential amino acids are: *arginine; cysteine; and tyrosine.*

The nonessential amino acids are: *alanine; aspartic acid; cystine; glutamic acid; glutamine; glycine; proline; and serine.*

Amino acids containing phosphorous need to be there for the *thymus*, which produces the *lymphocytes* (the disease-fighting white blood cells)   The right protein in adequate amounts is one of the most important steps in the growth and development of your dog.....and you too.

The amino acid, *tyrosine* is contained in protein foods (meat, poultry, fish, dairy products, and eggs). This amino acid stimulates the brain's production of *nor epinephrine* and *dopamine*, two alertness chemicals.   Your dog's mental alertness and overall energy can be elevated by his eating protein foods.

Beans provide the best source of vegetable protein, containing 41 to 45 grams per cup.   (Pinto, black and garbanzos.) Soybeans are a good formula for protein (20 grams per cup) containing all of the essential amino acids. Soybean products can be purchased at most health food stores and some pet supply stores in solid, liquid, and powder forms. It is available without carbohydrates or fats, providing 26 grams of protein per ounce.   Two tablespoons offer about the same protein as three ounces of T-bone steak.

There are two types of protein: (1) Complete, and (2) Incomplete. Each has different functions, and works in different areas of the body. Each has 4 calories per gram.

The *complete* protein provides the proper balance of eight necessary amino acids that build tissues, and is found in animal origin foods, such as meats, poultry, seafood, eggs, milk, and cheese. Cheese and eggs provide this protein without the heavy fats in meats.

The *incomplete* protein lacks certain amino acids, and is not used efficiently when eaten alone. Combined with small amounts of animal-source (complete) protein, it becomes complete. Grains, peas, beans, seeds, and nuts are sources of the incomplete protein. This can be just as nourishing, less expensive, and lower in fat than beef or pork. Be sure to use brown unrefined rice. The use of diets high in animal protein may be associated with increased risks of *heart disease and cancer*.

Remember: Your 7 to 8 week old puppy needs two-and-a-half times the amount of protein needed by an adult dog because growth needs protein, and your little guy is growing "like a weed." After 12 weeks, this need should drop to not more than twice the adult ration. Drop again at 6-months, to one-and-a-half times the adult need. By the time the puppy has grown to be no longer a puppy (one-year-old) a 25 pound canine companion can function well on 9 grams of protein per day. .

At 8 weeks, (if your puppy will weigh about 25 pounds at full growth) he probably weighs about 6 pounds now. He should have 5 grams of protein daily. Your 8 pounder at 12 weeks gets 6 grams daily. The double ration should be continued until the dog is a 9 month old, when it may be cut to 9 grams. It will stay at 9 grams until you companion is about 12 years old. Weigh your pet and follow chart number 2 for protein needs.

This book only considers the growth of your pet up to one year, which is the major growing time for your dog. No major change in diet is necessary until your companion reaches the middle-age of his life, about 12 years old, unless allergies or illnesses require a change.

To summarize, the consumption of complete proteins in your dog's diet, (meat, fish, poultry, cheese, eggs, and milk) contain ample amounts of all of the essential amino acids. Two incomplete proteins, such as rice and beans, become complete proteins when eaten together. (within a maximum time period of four hours).

The canine body responds to different proteins in various ways. Factors which are significant are: your dog's state of health; the food source of the protein: the digestibility of the food; the other nutrients taken with it; and its amino acid assortment. The most efficient protein use will be with carbohydrate, fat, and all of the necessary vitamins and minerals.

Malnutrition or infection can seriously impair digestion by reducing enzyme secretion. Absorption can be decreased by causing degeneration of the absorptive surface of the small intestine or losses from diarrhea. The cells' use of protein can be minimized by forcing amino acids to meet other needs. And infections cause an increased production of antibodies made of protein. Thus, malnutrition or infection make it harder to meet the increased needs of the pet.

If you choose not to include meat in your dog's diet, an alternative is to include cheese, eggs, or milk. But if you do not want to feed *any* foods taken from animals, you can mix and match plant products to obtain the numbers and balance of amino acids necessary to build his body protein. Meeting your pet's nutritional needs of protein is not difficult, unless the amount of food is greatly limited. If you wish, your dog can be a complete 'vegetarian' and still be healthy and nutritionally sound.

The absorption rate for the amino acids is better absorbed with animal proteins, however. (90 percent) Those coming from legumes are about 80 percent, and from grains and other plant foods vary from 60 to 90 percent. While cooking with dry heat tends to reduce protein digestibility, moist heat cooking usually improves it. The more nitrogen is retained, the higher the quality of the protein. This is the basis for determining the biological value of proteins. When nitrogen is negatively balanced muscle tissue is lost.

EXCESSIVE PROTEIN

Rather than too little protein, dogs eating commercial dog food will likely have too much protein. Animals who are fed high-protein diets may be prone to enlargement of the livers and kidneys, a protein overload effect. Many meats, which are high in protein, are also high in saturated fat.

Experiments have shown that animals fed high-protein diets show losses of zinc from their tissues, moreso as they age. Zinc loss has been linked to cognitive development deficit. Tests have shown a depreciation in mental abilities in human infants when their mothers were undernourished during pregnancy.

When the diet is too high in protein, deficiencies can also occur in calcium and vitamin B6. The more protein in the diet, the more calcium and vitamin B6 are needed. The calcium shortage depletes the bones of their primary mineral.

Dehydration can also be a result of too much protein. Water is needed to help excrete the wasted nitrogen. A racing dog trainer of greyhounds is especially concerned with water balance because performance is effected so much by it.

The results of the consumption of too much meat, which puts the dog's diet in protein excess, is observed by the professional groomer often. If the groomer is trained in nutrition, she will observe various symptoms:

* irritability	* red hives without pustules
* ulcerated joints	* rashes and flushed skin
* hot spots	* non-specific dermatitis
* strong urine	* crystals in the urine

The top professional groomers may be able to improve the skin problems, but many dogs may require veterinary care. Those who have urinary stones will definitely need to see a vet for allergy or 'itching' shots.

Dogs sometimes cause the 'excessive protein' problem by eating cat food. That seems to be one of the canine's fun-specials...stealing the cat's food. But his bad behavior tricks can backfire on him, because catfood is a much higher protein than dogfood. Cats require about 30 percent more protein than dogs. So by eating catfood, the canine thief upsets his nutritional balance...and has to pay the consequences...or you do.

PROTEIN REQUIREMENTS

Weight in Pounds	Adult Need Oz.	Puppy 7-11 Oz.	Puppy 12-25 Oz.	Puppy 26-52 Oz.
3	1	2.5	2	1.5
6	2	5	4	3
8	3	7.5	6	4.5
11	4	10	8	6
14	5	12.5	10	7.5
16	6	15	12	9
19	7	17.5	6	4.5
22	8	20	16	12
25	9	22.5	18	13.5

CHART 3

CHAPTER 5

CARBOHYDRATES

BRAIN FOOD FOR YOUR DOG

You want a smart dog? The dog's brain depends entirely on carbohydrate for its energy when available.

The energy of the sun's rays warming the green pigment *chlorophyll* in the leaves of a plant causes the carbon dioxide captured from the air by the leaves, and the water from the roots embedded in the soil, to combine into a simple sugar called glucose. This reaction is termed *photosynthesis.*

The first link in the food chain, carbohydrates support all living organisms on earth. Except for milk, in any appreciable amount, carbohydrates are derived from plants. If carbohydrates are deficient in your dog's diet, the canine's liver must substitute proteins for conversion to glucose. This puts an extra stress on the liver, and the protein's use for growth and cellular repair is compromised.

When we speak of carbohydrates in food, we are indicating starch and fiber, the complex carbohydrates. Simple carbohydrates, sugars, come in many forms: *fructose* (fruit and honey); *sucrose* (table sugar made through refining); *maltose* (malt sugar); and *lactose* (the sugar in milk).

One of the primary roles of carbohydrates, (sugars, starch, and fiber) which should make-up about 70 percent of your dog's diet, is to supply energy in the form of blood glucose. *Starch,* the main energy source of the animal body, is the most significant form of *glucose* (sugar) in the canine diet. Any of the other sugars can also supply glucose as well.

Dietary *fiber,* found in plant foods almost exclusively, is often referred to as roughage and bulk, and comes in two forms: water *insoluble* and water *soluble* fiber. Most plants provide both types.

Insoluble fiber is made-up of complex carbohydrates, but has no caloric value for dogs or humans. Ruminants, such as cattle, sheep, or deer, however, do digest it. Cellulose and lignin, the most common types of insoluable fiber, are found in fruit and vegetable skins, whole-grain foods including wheat bran, and some seeds.

The pulp of fruits, vegetables, and beans provide soluble fiber. Cereal products, such as oat bran are another source. Pectin, pentose polymers, some hemicellulose (widely found in plants and vegetables), and gums (found in the seeds and stems of some plants) are the most common types.

Insoluable fiber, which is a big part of most cereal brans, absorbs water as it moves through the small and large intestines, reducing stool bulk and transit time (the time it takes for ingestions to pass through the intestinal tract). This helps to normalize gut function and to dilute intestinal content, thereby preventing disorders resulting from abnormal muscular activity in the large bowel wall.

A different process takes place as soluble fiber (such as oat bran and beans) makes its way through the intestines. Stool bulk is also increased, but not so dramatically. The growth of normal intestinal bacteria, supported by the fiber, increases the bulk of colonic waste moreso. This fiber also protects against excess fats, just as potassium protects against excess sodium.

About .2 grams (one-fifth) of fiber per pound of adult body weight is optimal. So a 25-pound dog would need about 5 grams daily. A puppy should be brought up to this amount of fiber slowly. To elevate digestion of fiber too suddenly could constipate the dog. Stool formation will be a good gauge.

Carbohydrates, along with fats, provide a source of energy for dogs, who seems to have enough energy to light up a light bulb. Puppy needs carbohydrates in his daily diet so that the vital tissue-building protein is not wasted for energy when it might be needed for growth and repair. Carbohydrates have the same 4 calories per gram as protein.

There is a difference between humans and canines regarding the origin of the digestive process. In the human being digestion starts in the mouth, where the primary enzyme ptyalin in saliva initiates the digestive process by beginning a breakdown of the 3000 or so tiny glucose units in each molecule. But this does not happen with the canine digestive process. The dog's stomach is the first unit of digestion, but most digestion takes place in the small intestine.

Another digestive difference between the human and canine species is the mastication of food. Humans chew their food well, which, along with the enzyme action, sends the bolus of food into the stomach already partially digested. Dogs bolt down their food, using their teeth only for tearing the meat, and often swallowing chunks whole. Concerned pet guardians have lamented "I wish I could just teach Fido to eat more slowly and chew his food." But the dog is not a dainty, mannerly eater. Apparently, this has been an inherited trait which has remained from the wild-dog days, when packs of dogs attacked small animals for their food, and had to wolf-down the meat or be left without.

Indigestion has not been a big problem for canines, however. With strong digestive juices which can digest unchewed meat and bones, and the ability of a regurgitative action to expel those pieces too large, the dog's digestion is somewhat different than ours. When the bolus reaches the small intestine it is in about the same state as the humans.

But the all-meat, or heavy meat diet for dogs is not for the modern dog. We have learned that his primary dietary needs, just as is true of the human being, is for carbohydrates.

Brown rice is an excellent source of carbohydrate. However, carbohydrates should make up no more than 50% of the total calories for the day.

If your dog is expected to be 25 pounds when an adult, he will need 22.5 ounces of carbohydrates at that time. Your 8 week, 6 pound puppy needs 12.5 ounces daily. This should go up to 15 ounces daily when the little 8-pound guy reaches 12 weeks. Weigh your pet and go by the data on Chart Number 3 for his carbohydrate needs.

About 6 grams of fiber is necessary for dogs of all ages. Many diets will comply with this, but if the diet is low, add bran to the food. Bran can be purchased at health food stores. About a half-ounce of the more fiber-rich cold cereals can answer this need.

Read the labels and use a heavy fiber cereal.

CARBOHYDRATE REQUIREMENT

Weight in Pounds	Adult Dog Oz.	Puppy 7-11 Oz.	Puppy 12-25 Oz.	Puppy 26-52 Oz.
3	2.5	7	5	4
6	5	12.5	10	7.5
8	7.5	19	15	12.5
11	10	25	20	15
14	12.5	32	25	19
16	15	37.5	30	22.5
19	17.5	44	35	26
22	20	50	40	30
25	22.6	57	45	3

CHART 4

CHAPTER 6

F A T

THE GOOD & THE BAD

Fats are lipids. They are also called *triglycerides, fatty acids, esters* and *phosphatides*. There are three kinds of lipids: triglycerides; phosphatides; and *steroids*. The lipids in foods and in the canine body are 95 percent triglycerides, of which fatty acids are the major constituent and the chief form of fat. They may differ from one another in degree of saturation or chemical structure. Lecithin is a major *phospholipid*, and *cholesterol* is the best known steroid.

Stored in adipose cells beneath the skin and around the vital organs of the canine body, fat is supposed to cushion the organs and bones, providing insulation against cold and other dangers to the body. Fat cells are situated throughout the body of the canine, but are usually observed mostly in the area of the flanks and belly. Inwardly, excessive fat on the dog's body appears to be similar to raw chicken fat...yellow, translucent, and rather greasy.

Food fats such as triglycerides or cholesterol raise blood cholesterol in your pet. A high blood cholesterol over a period of time can be an indicator of cardiovascular disease. Thus, a high fat intake may cause heart problems with your canine.

There are two kinds of fatty acids: *saturated* and

unsaturated. Saturated fatty acids come from animal sources (meat, milk, eggs, and cheese). They are solid at room temperature. At 70 degrees Fahrenheit unsaturated fats are liquid...saturated fats are relatively solid.

A short chemistry lesson may be helpful here, to more fully understand the good and the bad of fat. Glucose, as was discussed in chapter 5, is the unit of energy useful to the body of the canine. When glucose is stored in fat, it is broken down into small molecules made up of carbon, hydrogen, and oxygen. Linked together into chains, these fragments are called *fatty acids.*

Fatty acids have different lengths of microscopic chains, and also possess various degrees of saturation. Chain length affects their solubility in water. Shorter chains are more water soluable. The more saturated a food---the more hydrogens in the fat, and the less it will melt at room temperature. If every available bond from the carbons is holding a hydrogen, the chain is a saturated fatty acid...filled with hydrogen.

Unsaturated foods are not filled with hydrogens. When one or more hydrogens are missing, there is an empty spot on the chain. When there is at least one point of unsaturation, the food is termed unsaturated...a monounsaturated fatty acid. When two or more points are unsaturated, it is a polyunsaturated fatty acid. When you see PUFA on an ingredient label, it refers to a polyunsaturated fatty acid.

We have known quite a bit about monounsaturate fatty acids for some time. But much more has been learned about the polyunsaturates *(linoleic...omega 6* and *linolenic...omega 3)* in recent years.. New knowledge about the linolenic acids has been acclaimed in the last few years. We now know that these two fatty acids are essential to the canine and human. We have known that linoleic acid (omega 6) was essential to the two species for some time, but only recently have discovered that linolenic (omega 3) is also essential to life...and that it cannot be synthesized by the body. It must be consumed as food. With omega 6 in the body, the other fatty acids can be made within...but not so with omega 3. A deficiency of omega 6 may show-up on your dog in the form a skin rash. And a shortage of omega 3 in your dog's diet will minimize bodily functions as well. When the intake of omega 3 is low, omega 6 will try to take it's place, but it's only a second- team player (maybe even a third). Production will be less.

Fish oil supplements can be substituted for foods containing omega 3 fatty acids, but there could be some problems if this is the only consumption of omega 3. Give your dog fish at least once-a-week... twice might be better. And add fish oil supplements at least once-a-week too. But more is not necessarily better. An excess can deplete the oxidant vitamins A, D, E, and K. Herring, mackerel, salmon, sardines, tuna, anchovies and whitefish are especially high in omega 3. Rated in the moderately high area are halibut, trout, smelt, bass, ocean perch, pollock, bluefish, mullet, and hake.

Unsaturated fatty acids, including mono- unsaturates and polyunsaturates, are usually liquid at room temperature. Unsaturated fats can also be derived from nuts, seeds, and vegetable sources.

Unsaturated fat helps to burn saturated fat, with intake balanced at 2-1. A minimum of one percent of the total caloric intake should include essential unsaturated fatty acids, commonly called vitamin F. Fats aid in growth and well-being by influencing glandular activity and making calcium available to the cells.

Stay away from butter, lard, and margarines because of the high saturation. Don't be fooled by the fallacy that margarine is okay. The hydrogenation processing of vegetable margarines causes them to be more saturated than the oils they are made from.

Unrefined, cold-pressed flaxseed oil is the best for omega 3 oils. About 57 percent of the oil is linolenic (omega 3); 16.16 grams per ounce. 16 percent is linoleic (omega 6); 4.54 grams per ounce. And 18 percent is oleic (monounsaturated); 5.1 grams per ounce.

Fat is needed by dogs to promote healthy skin and hair, but more specifically, fat is stored in the dog's body to provide energy at future times of need...for such bodily functions as: cell replacement; growth; repair; digestion; respiration, absorption, and metabolism; muscular use, including the heartbeat...and even the blinking of the eye. Your dog needs energy for each of a myriad of happenings within his body. Yes. He even needs energy to lie down in his bed.

Chemically, all of your dog's foods he eats have different combinations of atoms. Primarily, they are made up of carbon, hydrogen and oxygen, with smaller amounts of nitrogen, calcium, sulfur, and phosphorous. Food which is not used as energy can be changed into fat and stored, which indicates that ALL food may be fattening if too much is consumed. If your dog eats more of anything than his body needs, it will be converted to fat and stored for future energy use. Of course, if it is not used it becomes body fat. And, of each of the three basic kinds of food (proteins, fats, and carbohydrates), fat is easiest to store...and hardest to burn-off.

Fats contain more than twice the calories than either of the other two...nine to four. This means that a half-cup (4 ounces) of protein...or a half-cup of carbohydrate each contain approximately 450 calories, while the same measurement of fat has 1000 units of energy.

If your pet uses-up the same amount of calories as he takes-in, he will neither gain nor lose weight. If he needs to lose weight for optimal health, he will need to eat food containing less calories than he uses. This may entail both eating less and exercising more. If he needs to gain weight, he will have to take-in more calories than he uses-up through physical activity.

Fats also act as carriers for the fat-soluble vitamins A, D. E. and K, and help to make calciums available to body tissues, particularly in the teeth and bones by aiding in the absorption of Vitamin D. Fats add taste and a greater feeling of fullness after your pet consumes a meal.

Chart 4 refers to the fat requirements for your puppy. Since the requirements of fat are much lower in weight than the other major nutrients, the diet uses grams rather than ounces, which the charts on protein and carbohydrates used.

F A T

Weight in Pounds	Adult Dog Grams	Puppy 7-11 Grams	Puppy 12-25 Grams	Puppy 26-52 Grams
3	1.5	4	3	2
6	3	8	6	4.5
8	4.5	11	9	7
14	6	16	12	9
14	7.5	19	15	11
16	9	22.5	18	13.5
19	10.5	26	21	16
22	12	30	24	18
25	13.5	34	26	20

CHART 5

The 25-pound adult dog needs 13.5 grams of fat. The 8 to 12 weeks old puppy should have 6 grams unsaturated fat and 3 grams saturated.

Your 7 week old, 6 pound puppy needs 8 grams of fat daily. When he is at 12 weeks, the 8 pounder needs 9 grams of fat. At six months, the 13 pound puppy needs about 14 grams per day.

C H A P T E R   7

WHAT VITAMINS DOES YOUR BEST FRIEND NEED FOR WELLNESS?

Vitamins are present in the food our dogs eat. If the foods eaten don't provide adequate vitamins, we must supplement their diets with vitamins. Vitamins have no energy value themselves, but are vital to the metabolic function. Metabolism means the process of breaking down food for the body's use, converting that which is usable to energy and that which is unusable to waste, and eliminating it from the body. We, as well as our dogs, must have vitamins from foods or dietary supplements in order to sustain life. And it is impossible to continue living without all the essential vitamins.

METABOLISM: IMPORTANT WORD IN NUTRITION.

Write down the word "*metabolism.*" It is one of the most important words in the field of nutrition. It is taken from the Greek word "metabole," meaning change. Both your own and your dog's bodies need to chemically change food ingested, so that it can be used by the body.

The metabolism of proteins, carbohydrates, fats, vitamins, and minerals is essential before your dog's body can make use of nutrients. Various combinations and ratios are required in order to cause metabolism to take place, or to allow the body to make use of it. You will see this word often, as we survey the field of nutrition.

Vitamins are not a food *replacement.* They are a food *supplement.* A deficiency in even one vitamin can endanger the entire canine body. Each vitamin serves a distinct purpose which cannot be substituted. Vitamin supplements receive different reviews from those in the health field. Your pet can have a healthy body without adding vitamin and mineral supplements to the diet. This may not have been true fifty or sixty years ago, but it IS true today...for various reasons:

WHERE ARE THE VITAMINS?

What has happened in the last fifty years to change the need for supplements? Why must we supplement our food today in order to get enough vitamins? There are several answers to these questions.

Erosion of the soil.

Use of pesticides

Storage & refrigeration

Refinement/processing of foods.

Too much sugar, salt & fat.

Corporate formula for flesh marketing.

Food additives.

Hydrogenation

Preparation & service.

First, erosion of soil: the land has been stripped bare of nutrients by erosion, windstorms, floods, over-cultivation and under-fertilization for the past 200 years. Modern man has not given back to the soil what he took out.

Before modern man, there was a natural procedure of give and take--borrow and return. Animals lived on the produce of the land, storing it's minerals in their bodies, in their bones. They returned the minerals to the land through their excretions, and paid the debt in full when they died and returned to dust. And the cycle was continued for those following.

Modern man has not been so honest. He has accepted the earth's gifts without repayment. We've built sewers to take the excreta to the sea. We wrap our remains in a strongbox to keep the soil from reclaiming its minerals. We have taken from the soil sixty times what we have given back in fertilizer.

The density of nutrients in plants is reduced by the use of pesticides...used to *decrease* the soil organisms and *increase* the size of the crop...an economic maneuver, achieved at the expense of the consumer...both you and your dog.

When we pick foods before ripening and let them mature on freight cars, exposed to light and air. It is many days old when it reaches storage, and the cold storage depletes the food even more of its vitamins and minerals.

Processing and refining food renders already undernourishing foods negligible in vitamin-mineral content. The white, soft bread is a prettier product for the buyer, but the food value has been depreciated.

Today chemical pollutants also take a toll on the nutrient-content in food. The additives and coloring, used to make the food more appealing in appearance, further eradicate the real value of the food.

Sweeter and saltier food sells better, so food value is again sacrificed for economical gain. Fats add taste and satiety, so nutritional value is once more reduced in favor of sales value.

The food value of meat is also diminished by the manipulative actions of the corporate flesh marketers. Time is of the essence in modern-day animal growth. The rule is: The most weight in the shortest time.

A low protein/high carbohydrate continuous

overfeeding method fattens the cattle and pigs faster, enabling the corporation to turn the animals into money two or three months sooner than the family farmers had done many years ago.

Chickens, living in a small cage in a large shed, temperatures controlled, bright fluorescent lights illuminated continuously to encourage overfeeding, chemicals added, guarantees a plump chicken for the pot, in a shorter time. And time is money for these corporations in the food business.

Beef and pork sales are enhanced by the injection and ingestion of antibiotics, hormones, tranquilizers, poison copper sulfate, sodium pentobarbital, sodium nitrates, sodium nitrites, phosphates, and artificial smoke. The flesh gets a redder, more attractive appearance, and the bite is more tender, but you and your dog are not better-off for it.

Hydrogenation is a method of preventing spoilage of oils containing unsaturated fatty acids, which are vulnerable to oxygen. When oxidized the oils become rancid. Without hydrogenation, refrigeration is necessary to stop the oxidation process. But is is not practical or profitable for stores to keep everything refrigerated. Therefore, hydrogen is added to unsaturated fat, making it more solid, and changing the unsaturated fatty acids to saturated fatty acids. Obviously this is not a good choice for wellness, but a good one for marketing.

Then, if that isn't enough lowering of nutrition, the food is further dissipated when it is oxidized by heat and light through cooking. We pour out much of the remaining nutritional value in the water. It is estimated that up to 50-60% of our vitamins and minerals are lost before either human or canine bodies can use them.

Now, I believe, it is evident why we must supplement our food, both for ourselves and our dogs, with vitamin and mineral supplements.

I have been taking vitamins and minerals for many years before it was considered okay to do so. I was running and exercising back when other people looked at you as if you were some kind of nut. That may be why I feel that my actual physical age is about 20% below my chronological age. Both you and your dog can benefit from a lifestyle of wellness too.

You dog can look better, feel better, and live longer, if you make good use of this book...and so can you.

What are vitamins and what do they do for your dog? Most vitamins are natural substances found in foods, though they can be synthetically made. All natural vitamins are organic, and found only in living things, such as animals and plants.

Vitamins are either *water*-soluble or *fat*-soluble. Water-soluble vitamins pass through your pet's body in three to five hours, and therefore, must be replaced more often than once a day. Fat-soluble vitamins remain in the body for about twenty-four hours, though amounts can be stored in the liver for much longer.

Vitamins A, D, E, F, and K are the fat-soluble vitamins. Water-solubles are all the B vitamins, B complex, and C.

Vitamins do not add calories to the diet, nor do they provide energy themselves. They help to regulate metabolism (the body's use of food), converting carbohydrates and fat into energy.

Chemical analysis of both the synthetic and natural organic vitamins appear to be the same. Synthetic niacin, however, called niacinamide, can be taken easier than the organic niacin. Often niacin will cause a flushing and itching of the skin, while niacinamide will not.

Vitamins come in powder form for pets, as well as liquid

form, in many cases. Capsules can be opened up and put into the food, just as the dry form can. Tablets are usually more difficult to give dogs, but they can be given just the same as you would give medication in pill form. (See Chapter 10 .)

Vitamins can be mixed into the food. They can also be added to the pet's water. The food method is preferred, since the food is most often eaten in its entirety, while water may set for some time before being finished. And you might end up pouring the vitamins out when you put fresh water into the bowl.

Do not feed your dog vitamins on an empty stomach. It is best to space out the vitamins during the day. However, if you must give them only once a day, make it with the evening meal. Since vitamins are organic, they are absorbed best with food.

Be certain to give your dog minerals with the vitamins. Vitamins without minerals are *not* usable by his body.

Vitamin A, as well as D and E, require fats, as well as minerals, to be properly absorbed by the digestive tract. Since these vitamins are fat-soluable, and can be stored in the body, they need not be given every day.

Overcooking your dog's food can deplete vitamins and enzymes. The two variables involved in cooking food are time and temperature. A temperature of 99.7 degrees F is required for the breakdown of protein by chymotrypsin into polypeptides and amino acids. Therefore, some heat should be added to a meal in order to preclude excessive digestive system strain. The normal body temperature for dogs is 101 to 102, depending on age and other factors. Younger dogs tend to be at the higher level while older dogs are nearer the lower mark.

Mineral supplements should accompany vitamins for best utilization. Chapter 8 will teach you more about the minerals your dog needs.

Let us look at the vitamin needs of your dog.

VITAMIN A--HEALTHY SKIN AND HAIR; STRONG BONES AND TEETH.

Puppies need vitamin A (retinol or carotene) for development of growth, strong bones, teeth and gums. As they get older, healthy skin and hair become most important. The 8-to-12 week-old puppy needs 400 I.U.s daily. And when he is 3 months old, accelerate to 3000; then drop to 2000 at 6 month of age. As an adult, your dog should get 1500 I.U.s each day.

Liver is a good source of vitamin A. Desiccated liver can be purchased at the health food store. Carrots and green leafy vegetables are also high in vitamin A.

COD LIVER OIL IS HIGH IN 'A' & 'D'

Dogs don't get much vitamin D (calciferols) from the sun's ultraviolet rays since their skin is covered with hair. And since dogs cannot digest milk, and it often causes diarrhea, it should be removed from their diet, or reduced to no more than two ounces daily. Therefore, some vitamin D supplementation is necessary.

The casein in milk is not digestible by dogs. It turns to glue in the canine stomach. In fact, a large percentage of the human population have digestive problems with cow's milk too. Casein, a hard to digest protein, and lactose, the natural sugar in milk are the main culprits. In addition to the problem of digestibility, allergic reactions to milk also prevail frequently for both humans and canines.

Cod liver oil is an excellent source of vitamins A and D, while providing the essential fatty acids at the same time. One-half teaspoon gives your dog 200 I.U.s of vitamin D; 4000 I.U.s of vitamin A; 750 mg. Omega 3; and 50 mg. Omega 6.

This is sufficient in each of these nutrients for a daily requirement. The nutritious fish oil comes in different flavors at the health food stores too. It can be added to food or given by itself. It does not have to be given daily since it is fat-soluable. You could give one teaspoon once a week if you prefer. There are other forms of these oils found in most pet stores, as well.

You can put the oil in a capsule or in the food. You may also place the oil in the back of the dog's mouth, holding it shut a moment until he swallows. Massaging his throat will assist in swallowing. He will not like it at first, but he will get used to it. Your positive encouragement, such as "Oh, num-num-num. This is really good" may make the situation easier for both of you.

Do not assume that two are twice as good as one when giving your pet vitamins and minerals. Too much of any nutrient can upset the balance of other nutrients. This can be as bad or worse than too little.

An excess of unsaturated oils can precipitate a vitamin E deficiency, and in extreme cases, can cause heart problems.

Vitamin D is an aid to proper utilization of calcium and phosphorus. A deficiency of 'D' could cause calcium and phosphorus not to be utilized by the body, which would make your dog susceptible to brittle bones and teeth. However, once again, do not subscribe to the theory that twice as much is twice as good. Vitamin D in excess can be toxic...moreso that any other vitamin.

VITAMIN E (WITH SELENIUM) CAN MAKE YOUR DOG YOUNGER LOOKING

The third fat-soluble vitamin, which helps alleviate fatigue by assisting the supply of oxygen to the body, is best used by the canine when selenium accompanies it. Dogs with an adequate amount of vitamin E (tocopherols) and the mineral selenium often look younger than their chronological ages because oxidation is slowed down by a retarding cellular aging process. Vitamin E also enhances the activity of vitamin A.

Liver is a good source of vitamin E, as are green leafy vegetables, rice, millet, meal, bread, and other whole grains.

Desiccated liver can be added to your pet's meals to increase vitamin E consumption. Wheatgerm can also be sprinkled onto the meal, providing that your dog is not allergic to it. Wheatgerm is the fourth highest allergen food, after beef, milk, and yeast. See Chapter 9 for more on allergens.

Puppies 6-12 weeks need 50 I.U.s of vitamin E. Drop to 40 during the age of 13-25 weeks. Male dogs from six months of age need more vitamin E than females. Begin adding 10 percent for the males over the female's need at that time: 30 for the female; 33 for the male. The adult dog of a year old needs 22 I.U.s, while the female needs 20. And when the dog, male or female reaches 7 years of age, go back up to 30 I.U.s., in order to assist the age-retardation of your dog.

Vitamin K, a fat soluable vitamin needed by humans for blood-clotting, does not appear to be needed in food by canines. Like vitamin C, dogs make their own.

DOGS MAKE THEIR OWN VITAMIN C

Dogs synthesize their own vitamin C, while humans must rely upon dietary sources and supplements. Therefore, the vitamin C requirements for dogs is low. Unless the dog is afflicted with arthritis or hip dysplasia, he will need no supplements. In this case, 300 mg of C and 100 I.U.s of E may be needed. A nutritionally oriented vet should be consulted.

THE 3 MUSKETEERS: B1, B2, & B6

Thiamin, riboflavin, and pyridoxine, (B1, B2, & B6) should be equal in amount of need for the canine. The B vitamins are more potent when used together than individually. However, if any of them is higher in milligrams, it should be B6.

Adult dogs need 4 milligrams of each of these B vitamins. But start them off with 10 mg from 6-12 weeks; drop to 8 at 13-25 weeks; and 6 mg at 6 months to one year of age.

Thiamin, riboflavin, and pyridoxine can be obtained from meat, whole grains, peanut butter, blackstrap molasses, legumes, and nuts. Rice and lamb are a good combination. Sprouts, desiccated liver powder, cereals, and ground up nuts can be added to your dog's food to increase his B1, B2, and B6 consumption. Wheat germ is also a good source providing that your dog is not allergic to it.

THE MIGHTY-MITE B VITAMIN

Though your pet needs very little cobalamin, B12, a deficiency could result in mental or nervous disorders, low energy level, and poor fat, carbohydrate and protein utilization. The food sources of the vitamin, which is known for forming and regenerating the red blood cells, is generally the same as for the other B vitamins. Cheese is also a good source of B12.

The puppy, from 8 weeks to 6 months, needs 4 *micro milligrams*. After 6 months of age, drop to 3.

NIACIN...A CORTISONE SYNTHESIZER

Also known as vitamin B3, and one of the B complex family, niacin is essential for the synthesis of sex hormones (estrogen, progesterone, testosterone), as well as cortisone, thyroxin, and insulin. This vitamin is needed for healthy skin; helps to eliminate bad breath; increases circulation; reduces high blood pressure, and is necessary for a healthy digestive system.

Meats, whole grains, blackstrap molasses and legumes are good sources of niacin. Desiccated liver tablets or capsules are excellent in providing vitamin B3 also. The 6-12 week-old puppy should get 14 mg. daily. All others need just 7 mg.

B-COMPLEXES FOR SKIN & HAIR

All of the B complexes are necessary for dogs to keep a healthy skin and hair. A brittle, course hair, early graying, eczema, and other skin irritations can result with a deficiency of any of these important B vitamins. Some dogs, like humans, gray prematurely.

Folicin (folic acid), a member of the B complex family, which works along with vitamin B12 in the formation of red blood cells, is also one of the three having to do with the graying of hair. The others, which are synergetic with vitamins B2, B6, niacin, and vitamin A in maintaining healthy skin, are pantothenic acid and PABA. A deficiency can initiate dermatitis or eczema, and cause the impairment of fat metabolism. Biotin, another B complex vitamin that affects hair-graying with humans, is apparently not needed by the canine species. It is believed that they produce it themselves.

Lecithin, a lipotropic, which means that the prime function is to prevent abnormal accumulation of fat in the liver, is produced when combined with the mineral choline. Lecithin aids the thymus gland in stimulating the production of antibodies, which help the immune system leukocytes (white blood vessels) gobble up invading viruses and microbes, destroying them.

Though it is technically a mineral, choline is called the 'geriatric' B-complex vitamin because it has so much to do with aging diseases such as cirrhosis and fatty degeneration of the liver, and Alzheimer's disease, which we believe that some dogs go through. We know that some humans experience this malady. But because dogs cannot speak our language, we don't know that they can be afflicted with Alzheimers for certain.

Choline also helps control cholesterol build-up, which can cause arteriosclerosis; helps nerve impulses.

For the 8-12 week-old pup, 200 mgs are needed; 150 mgs for the 13-25 week-old; and 100 mg for the 6-month and older dogs.

Inositol, another of the B-complex group, like choline, is important in the nourishment of brain cells; effects skin and hair; metabolizes fats and cholesterol. Inositol requirements are the same as choline.

Tests which measure the values of B-complex vitamins, show the following results:

Human tests with patients who were suffering from senile dementia, exhibited dramatic improvement in their condition within 48 hours after taking B vitamins. (Beckness/Prescott, Vitamins in Medicine, 1973, Linda Clark)

CHAPTER 8

BUT DON'T FORGET THE MINERALS

We speak of vitamins frequently, and often say little about minerals. Therefore, a mineral deficiency may be more frequent than that of vitamins. But vitamins can do nothing with minerals. *Without minerals, vitamins are useless.* And, though the canine can manufacture some of its own vitamins, it cannot make a single mineral. And we repeat: vitamins cannot function without minerals present.

CALCIUM, PHOSPHORUS, & MAGNESIUM
THE BIG 3 MINERALS

Three of the most important minerals are calcium, phosphorus, and magnesium. This threesome needs to be in proper balance in order for minerals to have an optimal effect. In fact, if these three minerals are greatly out of whack, serious problems are just around the corner. Things don't happen immediately in the nutritional arena. It may take months...or even years, but life threatening problems will be there if these three minerals are not reasonably well balanced. This is one of the really big problems with mineral imbalance. Big meat-eaters cannot live a completely healthy and full-term life. Meat is so out-of-proportion with phosphorus that supplements of calcium and magnesium would need to be an enormous amount to counteract this imbalance. This is true in both the canine and human lives. The proper balance of the Big 3 is as shown below:

CALCIUM TO PHOSPHORUS 1.2 TO 1.0

CALCIUM TO MAGNESIUM 2.0 TO 1.0

Meat is about a 20 to 1 phosphorus-calcium ratio. It is therefore literally impossible to give your dog large amounts of meat and even come close to the necessary balance. Pet guardians who do this not only contribute to the UNWELLNESS of their dog, but take years off their lives. And the human is no different in this respect. The big meat-eaters die sick, and early.

Desiccated liver may be an answer for getting the nutritional values of meat, while not taking the phosphorus bombardment. It is dried at a low temperature, in a vacuum, so that most of the original nutrient value of liver is conserved in powder form. It is rich in calcium, phosphorus, iron, copper, and in vitamins A, C, D, and some B's. It can be added to baked goods, soups, and most any food.

Calcium and phosphorus work together for healthy bones and teeth, while calcium works with magnesium for cardiovascular health. Vitamin D, however, must be present for calcium to be absorbed at all. Calcium also helps metabolize your pet's iron intake.

MOLASSES IS A GOOD ADDITIVE FOR PETS

One tablespoon of blackstrap molasses has a calcium---phosphorus---magnesium ratio of 33-9-25. Since so many foods are highest in phosphorus, this is a good additive to foods, in order to boost the calcium and magnesium percentage.

The dark syrup-like food is excellent with rice, since rice is high in phosphorus. It is also rich in pantothenic acid, niacin, folic acid, vitamin E, potassium, and iron. Arthritis, dermatitis, hair damage, eczema, psoriasis, constipation, colitis, and nervous conditions may respond by supplementation of the diet with mineral-rich molasses.

Though brewers yeast is recommended by many, I

personally do not favor using it because of the very high phosphorus, and its propensity for allergic reactions. The flea prevention theory is merely a myth. It will not eliminate the flea problem for your dog.

For a year-old dog, a 300-250-150 mg ratio of calcium, phosphorus, and magnesium is a good one to shoot for. The 8-12 week-old puppy needs a higher phosphorus and magnesium ratio: 500-600-300. The 13-24 week-old adolescent should be 420-500-250 ideally. At 6 months, lower it again to 330-400-200 until your dog is a year old.

This Big 3 mineral balance is one of the most important fundamentals of good health for both your dog and you. With a puppy, you have the opportunity to start his life off right. But with a minerally-unbalanced diet, your dog will not enjoy his life as much...and he won't live as long as he might.

Kidney disease, which is the second leading killer among dogs, is most often caused by a high phosphorus diet of several years. Calcium and magnesium are thereby decreased. After about 6 years, your dog's kidneys no longer help to excrete the excess phosphorus, and calcium is again depleted. (Same for you after 40). Often one kidney goes first, just atrophies away...then the other one has to work twice as hard. It isn't long before the other kidney is gone. *Atherosclerosis*, caused primarily by the excessive saturated fat accumulated from heavy meat eating, the arteries filling up with cholesterol (fatty) deposits, is the ***number one cause of death for humans in the United States.*** *Phosphorus is needed in the bodies of dogs and humans...but only in balance with calcium and magnesium.*

STRESSED-OUT DOGS NEED MORE POTASSIUM

Potassium is needed in quantities of 670 mg daily for dogs 6 months to 6 years under normal conditions. If they live under stressful conditions, potassium should be increased to 737 (10%) to 804 (20%). The 8-12 week-old pup should be getting 1000 mg. At 13-24 weeks, 835 mg. The older dog should be at the 20% stress lever, 800+ mg.

An abnormally low or high blood sugar can cause a dog to need more potassium than under usual conditions, as can any mental or physical stress. Dogs left alone all day or who are fleas-infested, often need more potassium by 10 to 20 percent.

Potassium regulates the body's water balance and the normalization of heart rhythms. Potassium works inside of the cells, while sodium works outside of the cells. If the potassium-sodium balance is off, the nerve and muscle functions can suffer. Salting your dog's food a little is import too...but don't overdo it. Potassium further helps dispose of body wastes, aids in allergy treatment, and assists in reducing blood pressure. Too much sodium can raise the blood pressure.

Manganese helps to activate enzymes necessary for body's proper use of vitamins B1 and C. It is also needed for normal bone structure, assists with digestion and food utilization, and is considered important in mental order and memory.

For the 8-12 week-old puppy, 300 mg of manganese is proper. At 13 weeks to a year, 250 mg. After a year-old to about 12 years, drop to 150 mg. But after 12, it should increase again about half. Older dogs sometimes show confusion and mental disorder. Dogs should not have to get senile...and neither should their guardians if attention is paid to diet, exercise, and controlling stress.

If you follow this effective program from early in your dog's life, you will likely eventually see a dog past 20 who is still reasonably well. But remember, we cannot undo in a few weeks or months what we did to cause the problems over many years.

KEEP FRESH WATER AVAILABLE
TO YOUR DOG AT ALL TIMES.

Iron is necessary for the production of hemoglobin (red blood corpuscles) and other enzymes. Copper, cobalt, part of B12, manganese, phosphorus, and iron are necessary for proper metabolism of the B vitamins, as is phosphorus and zinc.

The 8-12 week-old pup need 18 mg of iron daily. Cut to 16 at 13 weeks; then to 12 at 6 months. Liver, fish, and blackstrap molasses are good iron sources.

Copper is needed for iron to work. Copper aids in iron absorption, keeps the energy level up, and assists iron in hemoglobin production. It also makes the amino acid tyrosine work. Just a half milligram of copper is necessary for the 6-week-old pup. You can raise it to 4 mg at 6 months, then drop to 3 mg for the year-old adult dog.

Zinc is one of the most often deficient mineral for both dogs and humans, unless supplemented. The depreciation of nutrients from our farm lands has depleted the zinc ordinarily present in foods. Therefore, *zinc must be supplemented for both humans and canines.*

Zinc is essential for the synthesis of protein; governs the contractibility of muscles; helps in the formation of insulin; stables the blood; maintains the body acid-alkaline balance; influences brain function; acts as a traffic cop, directing the efficient flow at body processes; facilitates the release of vitamin A from the liver; controls the toxicity of cadmium; is required for B complex's absorption and actions; helps metabolate phosphorus; and assists copper and cobalt in food digestion.

For your dog's zinc needs, feed him soybean products,

liver, fish, legumes, and peanut butter (or ground-up nuts). The 12-week to 6-month-old dog gets 10 mg; at 6 months to a year, 10 mg; and cut to 5 mg after a year of age.

Zinc is more important to males since it affects the prostate gland.

Selenium is synergistic with vitamin E. They work together in metabolic and growth functions. The two together are stronger than the sum of the equal parts. They are both antioxidants, and slow down aging and tissue hardening.

Males need twice the amount of selenium as females since we know that almost half of their body's supply concentrates in the testicles, and seminal ducts near the prostate gland. If your male adult dog is in stud, increase his selenium and zinc at least ten percent. Selenium is lost in semen. We know that selenium also has an effect on the skin. A shortage often produces dandruff or flaking skin.

Females should had .1 mg daily throughout the dog's life. Double it for males. Liver, molasses, whole-grain bread, and fish are good sources for dogs.

Iodine promotes proper growth, healthy hair, nails, skin, teeth. It helps to give more energy, and burns fat. In older dogs a deficiency can be responsible for mental deterioration.

If your dog is getting iodized salt, chances are he is getting enough iodine. He needs about .05 mg. through his first year. The adult dog needs .02 mg.

Chromium helps to bring protein to where it is needed, aids growth, works with insulin in the metabolism of sugar, and helps to prevent and lower high blood pressure. The puppy should have .05 mg daily, continuing through the first year. Older dogs should increase to .075 mg. If your dog has diabetes, the amount should be increased to 1 mg.

Blackstrap molasses and liver are again a source. Whole grain cereals, breads, clams, and corn oil will provide some chromium.

CHAPTER 9

FOOD ALLERGIES
MISERY & DEATH

Those veterinarians who have some nutritional training fully agree that over half of the sick animals brought into their veterinary clinics are there largely because of an improper diet...food related.

One such veterinarian wrote a book called "Pet Allergies." Alfred J Plechner, D.V.M., did not start out with much nutritional knowledge. He acknowledged that he had been practicing for five years before he realized that most of the sick animals who came into his office had food allergies, and that these allergies caused a major number of these medical problems.

Dr. Plechner said that he thought that he must have missed part of his veterinary training. He did not recall any academic study on the problem. He had to study on his own to learn a great deal more in order to diagnose these allergy problems.

As Plechner tried to treat his patients with standard treatments that he had learned in his profession, results were not satisfactory. He writes *"I took continuing education courses, read all of the available literature, but got little help."* He suspected that allergens were a major cause of the problems faced. In time, he came to the conclusion that many cases with widespread clinical signs related directly to the animal's food.

The doctor was seeing a great deal more than just the symptoms of food sensitivities such as itching and scratching, usually attributed to this. He observed such things as kidney ailments, liver problems, epilepsy, and other serious ailments. The pet nutritional pioneer set out to design a plan to help pet guardians to deal with food allergies.

After over 30 percent of his patients were responding to treatment, either partially or totally, Dr. Plechner realized that he had made an amazing discovery. He further learned that many of the commercial foods for pets were grossly inadequate.

Plechner said *"I frankly feel that much of the commercial pet food on the market is so alient, so multiply altered, so chemical-laden, that only the strongest of animals can remain healthy on it over a lifetime."*

Further, after revealing that by-products include feathers, beaks, waste material, fecal matter, skin with hair, rejected matter, and more, he states, *"By products often make-up a big part of the total protein. Your animals utilize such ingredients poorly, if at all. The diseased tissue, pus, hair, assorted slaughterhouse rejects, and carcasses in varying states of decomposition are sterilized with chemical, heat, and pressure procedures. Then crafty processing techniques are applied to fashion food that tastes and looks good. Finally, product labels are written by shrewd merchandisers who hide more than they tell."*

The veterinarian says that *"the poor quality excessive protein over the long run is **a prescription for kidney disease**. The dog's internal organs are incapable of handling these impurities, and the kidneys become inflamed, damaged, irritated, and deteriorated after several years of life. When the kidney ceases to function, it may atrophy, putting all of the load on the second kidney, until it can no longer withstand the*

68

bombardment of unwholesome filth. "

After over 20 years of practice, the caring vet has made some amazing discoveries. Because of these enlightening revelations, he is now one of the foremost leaders in the field of pet allergies, and most likely has much to add to the curriculum to be studied by future aspiring veterinary students.

But the commercial dog food industry is not the whole problem in the food allergy dilemma. Dogs are allergic to many, many foods. And they are allergic to some foods at certain times of the year, and not at other times...and with certain combinations of food.

The early symptoms are usually itching, scratching, biting, and licking various parts of their bodies. This is indeed uncomfortable and stressful to the dog. And most guardians think it is fleas causing the problem. But the really serious final outcome is often **grave sickness and death.**

BEEF, MILK, & YEAST.....3 BIG ALLERGENS

Meat is one of the biggest of all foods that cause allergies. **Beef is the number 1 allergy producer.** Milk is also a highly ranked allergen. Few dogs can tolerate cows milk.

Here is the **"Allergic hit list"** as devised by Dr. Alfred J. Plechner over two decades of study:

1. beef and beef byproducts
2. milk
3. yeast, including brewers yeast
4. wheat, wheat germ, and wheat germ oil
5. corn and corn oil
6. pork
7. turkey
8. eggs

You can test your dog for allergic reactions to any food by simply eliminating one food at a time from his diet for a week. If allergic-like reactions are reduced, you may be able to determine which foods cannot be tolerated. Then put a stop to allergic symptoms by removing that food from his diet. Another method is discussed in this chapter below.

STAR-TREK COMMANDER
LEARNS ABOUT ALLERGIES

One of the California veterinarian's cases was 'Heidi,' a 5-year old Doberman, whose guardian was actor Bill Shatner, most well-known for playing Captain Kirk in the Star Trek television series and movies. The star's dog had been in a great deal of pain, and the Shatner's usual veterinarian had diagnosed the ailment as a spinal condition, which affected the dog's legs. The vet had advised the Shatners that the dog should be put to sleep.

Dr. Plechner was called-in for a second opinion. From his examination, Plechner suspected a food allergy. After two weeks on a non-meat diet, the dog was walking normally and feeling well.

The pain and leg dragging had been caused by a severe intestinal reaction to beef, and she had been bloated with gas, with a severely distended abdomen. This caused her to drag her hind legs from the pain, and to appear paralyzed, which is indigenous to a disc disease, for which dogs are put to sleep.

The original veterinarian's diagnosis was a mistake because he did not know enough about nutrition and food allergies. Heidi, who had been well cared for as far as the Shatners thought, had been on a steady diet of high-grade beef all of her life. The famous guardian thought that he was feeding his dog very well, with a steady diet of fillet-mignons and other highgrade meats every day. It took five years for Heidi's body to finally cry out. She could take it no more.

After three months on a non-meat diet, Marci Shatner, Bill Shatner's wife, reported to the vet that the dog was frolicking around with the vigor of a puppy, with an improved coat and a rejuvenated personality.

Heidi enjoyed good health until she died at the age of 14. Most likely she would have lived a longer life, had she been on a low-meat diet all of her life... most certainly a less painful one.

Heidi's problem was one of innocent ignorance on the part of her famous guardians, and a lack of knowledge on the part of the first veterinarian. Neither of them was well enough informed.

Such a mistake for laymen is understandable. For centuries, we had believed that dogs must have meat...that they are meat-eaters.

MILK DOESN'T ALWAYS "DO-A-BODY-GOOD"

Much has already been said about milk as a "no-no" in the dog's diet. The textbooks on human food allergies list milk as the highest rated of all foodstuffs in the causes to allergic reactions. And those studies say that at least 75 percent of all dogs fed cow's milk will develop one or more allergies. Headaches are one result of an allergic reaction to milk. Of course dogs get headaches too.

Neither canines nor humans are physiologically able to digest any milk except for the the milk from the mother. And even then, only for 6 weeks (canines) and 3 years (humans). The enzymes rennin and lactase, needed to breakdown and digest milk, are no longer in the body by these ages.

We discussed milk in Chapters 2 and 5, and we know that *"Every body does not need milk."*

Our past assumption that 'puppies, after weaning, need

71

cow's milk because they had been on a diet of milk from their canine mother,' is obviously a wrong one. But there is a multi-billion dollar industry out there with millions of dollars spent on advertising annually. The continuous 'hard sell' on the values of milk is everlasting, and it's pretty hard to buck the picture of an attractive child or healthy appearing youth smiling, drinking a glass of milk. "It does a body good." the ad says. To contest that is almost like defiling the flag, defacing the statue of liberty, or separating mom and apple pie.

THE MYTH ABOUT YEAST

Brewer's yeast, though high in vitamin B1, is inadvisable for use with dogs because of the high phosphorus-to-calcium content. But it is doubly inadvisable because of its high rate of allergenic reaction by dogs. The common myth that it is an inhibitor of fleas for dogs has propelled it into popular use.

The reason yeast is said to work as a repellent is because the yeast gives off an odor when it gets into your sweat glands, and this odor is not to the liking of fleas. Your dog has these sweat glands only between his toes. Dogs have no sweat glands on their bodies, except between the phalanges. Yeast can also cause the capillaries under the skin to expand. This may cause hot spots and itching which can make the pet very uncomfortable and susceptible to flea infestation.

Wheat and corn are often the largest ingredients in many pet foods. The grains add bulk and are cheap fillers. These grains can be allergenic to dogs. Wheat germ, wheat germ oil, and corn oil can cause allergic reactions too.

Eggs can be allergenic to your dog, particularly the white of the egg. Some dogs can even experience a facial swelling.

The motivator of an allergic reaction for your dog may be determined by a tedious process of elimination, or by going

72

to a strictly hypoallergenic diet, such as rice, then adding another food each week. Since rice is about the least allergenic of grains, and is a good carbohydrate source, it can be a good food to start with. It's high phosphorus content however, makes it necessary for you to add calcium and magnesium to it. Blackstrap molasses, yogurt and cheese will bring up the calcium and magnesium, but add these carefully, individually, as you continue to find the culprit or culprits causing the allergic reaction. Powdered calcium and magnesium should be added if the totals do not balance.

By using rice as your 'base' diet, then adding foods one at a time, you may be able to find the causing agent. You can give the rice some taste by adding some blackstrap molasses, garlic, cinnamon, or other spices. Be sure to use the brown, unrefined rice. If the symptoms go away on the rice diet, start your efforts to find the mystery agent. If the symptoms haven't returned in a week, you're home free on that one. Then go on to the next food.

If you try meat, try lamb first. It is the least allergic of all meats. You can grind it up, cook it in safflower oil or olive oil, and add it to the rice easily. But the high phosphorus content of both rice and lamb signify that you need to add calcium (alot) in order to retain a proper calcium-phosphorus-magnesium ratio.

Be sure to eliminate anything else that could cause an allergic reaction, such as chew sticks and treats. Even a bite can set a dog off, reacting to an allergen. You should also feed abit more sparingly, so as not to overload his digestive system.

If the allergic symptoms are not eliminated with food restriction there can be other allergic causes such as carpets, wool, cats, red dye in his dish, plastic toys, etc. Breeding imperfections can also cause allergy-like symptoms.

CHAPTER 10

ALTERNATIVE NUTRITIONAL THERAPIES TO INSURE WELLNESS & LONGEVITY FOR YOUR DOG . . . & YOU TOO.

Effective monitoring of your dog's food, insuring that he eats the proper foods...does not eat the foods he shouldn't... balancing his nutrients...and supplementing his nutritional needs with vitamins and minerals are all vital to establishing optimal wellness and longevity. But keeping your dog well, the best-he-can-be, and reaching maximum longevity will likely not be possible without the use of three more health therapies: *herbs; cellular therapy; and enzyme therapy.*

HERBAL

Herbal medicine is the most ancient health care method for all cultures known to civilization...existing since the beginning of life on earth. The oldest recorded systems of herbal medicine appear to be in China, India, and Egypt.

Emperor Shen-nung, said to have had a transparent stomach, and lived over three-thousand years before Christ, recorded in the *Pen-ts'ao* 314 herbal medical preparations. Modern historians, however, have placed Shen-nung in the first millennium before Christ. Taoists, from 300 years B.C., to 700 A.D. believed in disease prevention through moderation, using acupuncture, herbs, diet, massage and light exercise.

In India the medical system is known as Ayurveda, the

science of life. Though claims indicate that the system goes as far back as 10,000 B.C., written records authenticate the time at around 1,000 B.C. Herbs are a large part of Ayurveda, which dimished somewhat due to political turmoil at about 1200 A.D. Recorded in the first century A.D., the *Charaka Sambita* mentions 500 herbal drugs.

The Egyptians also developed herbal-based medical practices at about the same time as the Chinese and Indians. The *Papyruses*, which go back to about 2000 B.C. refer to older traditions of herbal medical uses.

Through Greco-Roman and the Persian Empire times, for the next two-thousand years, herbs continued to be used by the physicians to cure diseases and afflictions. The first 1500 years A.D. saw the use of herbs as the primary medical use. *Gerald's Herbal*, published in 1597, listed 1.000 herbal species.

The discovery of America brought the colonists, to whom herbs were as important as the vegetables in their gardens. In 1633, *The Herbal* listed 2.850 herb plants. And in 1640, 3,800 herbs were covered in *Theatrum Botanicum*.

But the rising of *orthodox* medicine created a decline of herbal use, as *blood-letting, cathartics, and purgatives* created a decline in the population. Orthodox medicine improved, however, as blood-letting advanced to surgery, and more became known about the human and animal bodies. Physicians and veterinarians today are necessary practitioners in the health field. But there is a stronger growth of herbal medicine, and new professions in alternatative medicine have been born which incorporates orthodox, herbal and other health practicioners:

acupuncturists	**chiropractors**
homeopaths	**nutritionalists**
naturapaths	**nutritionalists**
herbalists	

An herb may be a seed, root, leaf, flower, or a stem, fruit, bark, or any such plant part which is used for medicine, food flavoring, or fragrancies. There are believed to be as many as a 500,000 plants on earth today. And only about one-percent of them have been studied extensively for applications to the presevation of health.

The botanical medical application, which is also called phytotherapy or herbal medicine, has endured since time began. And though economics is the main reason for the demise of the use of pure herbs for medicine by the medical physicians in the United States, many herbs are still used in pharmaceutical medicines. But since herbs cannot be patented, there can be be exclusive rights of herb ownership by the drug companies. Therefore, these companies are not prone to invest in testing or promotion of herbs. Americans are conditioned to think "cure," rather than "prevent." Most have not realized that a cure would not be necessary if they took pains to retain wellness. And the medical profession has made little effort to change that attitude. The multi-billion dollar pharmaceutical drug corporations have controlled the medical profession. As stated earlier...*economics is the word.*

But there appears to finally be a change in the making. The American public has become greatly concerned over pharmaceutical drug side effects, and the impersonal, almost lackadasical attitudes among the medical profession toward their patients. They are also becoming extremely pessimistic about the high costs of health care, including physician/veterinary fees, hospital charges, insurance, and drugs. And they are becoming more suffisticated about alternatives...reading more, giving attention to television health programs, and learning more. They are learning what herbs really are, and what they can do. The World Health

Organization (WHO) has brought out that about three-quarters of 119 plant-derived pharmaceutical medicines are now used in modern medicine...and in the same way they were used as 'medicines' by earlier cultures. Herbs have-been, and are-now used for everything in health from stress-reducing teas to powerful drugs. And, after centuries have passed, the people are returning to the use of herbs...for themselves and their animals.

Herbs come in several different ways:

Whole Herbs are all or part of plants which are dried and cut.

Bitter Herbs are put in capsules for easy swallowing.

Extracts allow for space-concentration, and quick assimilation.

Essential Oils also offer space-concentration.

Salves, Balms, Gels, Ointments are effective for skin problems. If your dog does not like the taste of an herb, put it in an empty capsule and place it in the back of his mouth...close his mouth with your hand...rub his throat with the other hand, while holding his mouth shut. He will swallow it.

A nutritionist who works with dogs, or a veterinarian who is knowledgable about nutritional needs should be consulted. Certainly, prevention is prefered to cure. By an intelligent use of herbs, you may be able to keep your pet well...and not need a cure.

The herbs below are listed according to general-uses. Dosage should be according to weight. Directions on health store bottles are usually based on a weight of about 150 pounds. Dose accordingly for your dog's weight. And be aware of any dangers to health which may be caused by some herbs in excessive dosage.

AGING

Gota Kola; Ginkgo Biloba; Siberian Ginseng; Dandelion Leaf;

ALLERGIES

Echinacea Root; Bayberry Bark; Plaintain Leaf; Myrrh Gum; Garlic; Horehound; Fenugreek; Eyebrite; Black Cohash; Lobelia; Ephedra; Nettle.

ARTHRITIS

Ginkgo Biloba; Alfalfa; Burdock; Capsicum; Kelp; White Willow Bark; Witch Hazel; Sasparilla Root; Saffron; Valerian Root; Prickly Ash Bark; Mugwort; Mullein Leaf; Oregon Grape Root; Prince's Pine; Feverfew; Hydranga Root; Ginger.

CIRCULATION...HEART...BLOOD

Ginkgo Biloba; Pau d' Arco; Capsicum; Bayberry Bark; White Oak Bark; Siberian Ginseng; Skullcap; RootDamiana Leaf; Golden Seal Root; Kelp; Hyssop; Alfalfa; Dandelion Root; Yellow Dock Root; Thyme; Garlic; Barberry Bark; Chamomile Flower; Burdock Root; Hawthorn;Burdock Root; Echinacea.

CONSTIPATION

Gota Kola; Aloe Vera; Slippery Elm Bark; :Peppermint Leaf; Witch Hazel Bark; Blackberry Leaf; Buckthorn Bark; Cascara Sagrada Bark; Oregon Grape Root; Mandrake Root; White Oak Bark; Senna; Rose Hips; Yellow Dock; Blue Flag.

DIGESTION...FLATULENCE

Fenugreek; Aloe Vera; Nettle Leaf; Cascara Sagrada Bark; Slippery Elm Bark; Papaya Leaf; Peppermint Leaf; Balmony; Gentian Root; Bay Leaf; Marjoram; Alfalfa; Rosemary;

Angelica Root; Lobelia; Capsicum; Fennel Seed; Garlic;
Camomile Flower; Blessed Thistle; Golden Seal; Passion
Flower; Peppermint; Ginger; Centuary; Sage; Cinnamon;
Juniper Berries; Anise; Basil; Chervil; Thyme; Sweet Cicely.

ENERGY

Astragalus; Siberian Ginseng Root; Fo-Ti; Damiana Leaf;
Capsicum; Kola Nut; Echinacia Root.

HEMORRHOIDS

Aloe Vera; Buckthorn Bark; Burdock Root; Myrrh Gum;
Yarrow; Ursi Leaf; Witch Hazel; Elderberry; Echinacia.

IMMUNE SYSTEM

Pau d' Arco; Echinacea; Ginseng; Tropical Periwinkle;
Astragalus; Flaxseed Oil; Purslane; Shizandra; Genseng.

KIDNEYS & BLADDER

Camomile; Alfalfa; Barberry Bark; Black Cohosh; Capsicum;
Chamomile Flower; Dandelion Root; Ephedra; Goldenseal;
Chervil; Uva Ursi; Pipsissewa; marshmallow; Lovage.

LIVER...PANCREAS...GALL BLADDER

Ginkgo biloba; Milk Thistle; Dandelion Root; Celandine;
Rosemary; Sweet Woodruff; Oregon Grape; Indigo; Barberry;
Gentian Root; Feverfew; Blessed Thistle; Agrimony; Turmeric.

PARASITES (exterior)

Pennyroyal Herb Extract (mix 1 fluid ounce with 20 ounces of
water in a 20 ounce spray bottle. Spray on dog (external use
only); Garlic for intestinal worms; Anise; Southern Wood.

PROSTATE

Corn Silk; Saw Palmetto; Damiana; Parsley; Buchu; Kelp..

RESPIRATORY

Mullein Leaf; Colts Foot; Fenugreek Seed; Nettle Flower;
Myrrh Gum; Ephedra; Betony; Bloodroot; Poplar; Eucalyptus.

SKIN

Aloe Vera; Dandelion Root; Marigold; Eucalyptus; vinegar.

CELLULAR THERAPY

Cell Therepy is the infusion of healthy cellular material from organs, embryos, and fetuses of animals into the body, in order to regenerate old or diseased cells. The method of infusion may be by injection, or oral (swallowing dried cells in a capsule). If the human or canine is seriously ill, such as in cancer, diabetes, arthritis, etc., the injection method may be used. However, if the problem is not a degenerative disease, the oral method is acceptable. For the dog owner, oral inception is administered by a veterinarian, a nutritionalist, or the pet's guardian. Health food stores stock the dried glandulars in capsule form.

How do these whole cells infiltrate to their intended destination? Through the process of ultrafiltration. The cell surface coat and its antigenic material are removed. Cells are broken down to their molecular levels, and find their way to the patient's weak or damaged organ. The body's healing process is stimulated, and without error, the cells migrate to their places of need, ie. liver cells to the liver...pancreas cells to the pancreas, etc.

ENZYME THERAPY

Digestion and absorption must take place in an animal or human organism in order for life to continue. Enzymes provide the stimulus for every chemical reaction in the animal or human body. Without enzymes, vitamins, minerals, and hormones cannot function. Proteins, carbohydrates, and fats must have enzymes to do the work...plant enzymes strengthen the digestive system...pancreatic enzymes help the digestive system, but also aid the immune system. The various enzymes are designed to act upon a specific organ through the acidity evident in that organ. Enzymes are functional only in their specific organ. So an enzyme active in the stomach will not work in the mouth, etc.

Absorption of the nutrients from the proper foods your dog eats is the key to good health. If he does not eat the proper foods...or he eats proper foods, but they are not absorbed...his body will react negatively...illness occurs. When the stomach is doing it's job, and the food is not cooked heavily, the food will be partially digested when the bolus arrives in the stronger digestive juiced stomach. For this reason, a good portion of your dog's food should be raw. (Yours too.) **Cooked food has no enzymes. Heat destroys enzymes at about 118 degrees.** When the body receives few enzymes, metabolic harmony is sacrificed, and the body systems are weakened.

Food is predigested by plant enzymes in the stomach, which allows the food to be partially digested when it arrives in the stomach. Fewer of the internal digestive enzymes are needed to digest the food since it has already been partially digested. It takes a half hour to an hour for the hydrochloric acid (HCI) to accumulate in the stomach to start digesting food.

This means that there is less work for the stomach enzymes and the HCl to do. Then the enzymes are not destroyed by the acidic environment, but merely deactivated. Later, the enzymes are reactivated in the duodenum in the more alkaline pH. If this idealic situation takes place, the food can be digested in the stomach in less than an hour.

When the body *does not* take-in enough enzymes, such digestive system problems as: toxic colon, inflammations, pancreatic hypertrophy, and allergies can occur. Inflammation can further incite such conditions as bronchitis, sinusitis, cystitis, rhinitis, and arthritis. The presence of fever, redness, swelling, and pain is telling you what is occuring. A meal which is made-up of all cooked foods may also increase the white blood count, which indicates that the immune system is being put into service. This is called digestive leukocytosis, which occurs about 30 minutes after eating cooked foods. When raw food is eaten, this does not occur because of the plant enzymes present. When digestive problems have been cleared up, often many other problems disappear too.

For these reasons, a quarter to a third of your dog's diet should be raw foods. (Yours too.) The *shredder and grater* are important tools to use when preparing your dog's food. Carrots, cabbage, beets, and onions are good vegetables to shred or grate into the other foods. For fruits, prepare apples, pears, peaches, lemons, oranges, bananas, papayas, and pineapples.

Some vegetables (avacados, peas, and beans and fruits (grapes, blueberries, and figs) may be sliced or mashed. Foods such as spinach or lettuce may be torn in pieces.

Pancreatic enzyme therapy promotes health by supplementing the body's own pancreatic enzymes...thereby lowering the demands on the body, since the body does not have to supply as many enzymes to convert food to nutrients and energy. The immune system is directly assisted by this conversion process. This function offers a significant example of the therapeutic powers of these enzymes.

It is suggested that the protein molecules, though being only partially digested in the small intestine, are able to be absorbed into the bloodstream. The immune system, thinking that they are foreign invaders, gives-off antibodies to counteract the supposed invaders by forming circulating immune complexes (CICs). If the body is a well, the CICs are neutralized in the lymphatic system. But if the body is unwell, the CICs stagnate in the blood, where they may set-off an allergic reaction. If the kidneys are unable to excrete all of them, an accumulation takes place in the soft tissues, inflammation is evident, and the immune system is stressed unnecessarily.

Pancreatic enzymes break down the CIC's, enabling them to pass through the kidneys for excretion. Pancreatic enzymes can digest foreign proteins, and remove infecting organisms such as viruses, scar-tissue, and inflammation.

Enzymes are able to initiate reaction that can digest the protective protein coat of viruses, enabling the virus to be destroyed. Cic's, which are abundant in viral disease, can also be hampered by enzymes.

The body uses inflammation as a response to noxious stimuli in an effort to rid itself of harmful substances. Pain, redness, swelling, and heat are the classic signs of inflammation. But the inflammation is helpful because it brings on healing.

Europe has led the way in enzyme therapy. Its future seems to be assured. The field, which now has over 2000 enzyme therapists, is expanding rapidly. It appears that enzyme therapy, cell therapy, and herbal medicine will be well represented in nutrition and prevention of chronic degenerative disease for both humans and canines for years to come.

CHAPTER 11

A RECIPE FOR WELLNESS AND LONGEVITY

Proper food for your dog can have a great deal to do with flea infestation too. Fleas prefer to find an animal who is the least resistant to be their unwilling host. A dog who is under stress from eating poor commercial pet foods, or an otherwise inefficient or poorly balanced diet is indeed more vulnerable to pests. A dog who is low in minerals provides the flea with an attractive 'free meal.' But minerals affect the blood. So control fleas with a balanced, nutritional, mineral-supplemented diet.

A balanced diet is also a deterrent to dental problems. Dental difficulties can also have a poor effect on your dog's overall health.

KNOW WHAT YOUR DOG SHOULD NOT EAT.

No, or little **milk**

Little **meat**

No **yeast**

No raw **egg white**

Poor **commercial dog foods**

BALANCE THE MAJOR NUTRIENTS

Keep the **carbohydrates** at about 50 percent.

Fat should not exceed 30 percent of the diet.

Protein needs to be about 20 percent.

Give your dog the vitamins and minerals he needs for the dog's **age, size, and gender.** Remember to balance the Big 3 minerals at: **Calcium 1.2 to Phosphorus 1.0**
Calcium 2.0 to Magnesium 1.0

P O W E R   F O O D   L I S T
(In alphabetical order)

ACIDOPHILUS

Acidophilus is a source of friendly intestinal bacteria, and more effective than yogurt. When a pet is taking antibiotics, the beneficial intestinal flora can be destroyed, often causing diarrhea as well as an overgrowth of fungus. These fungi can grow in the intestines, vagina, lungs, mouth, and under the nails. Acidophilus culture in the proper amounts will usually destroy the fungus growth in a few days. The friendly bacteria will last only about 5 days, so they need to be replenished.

BLACKSTRAP MOLASSES

Good calcium-phosphorus-magnesium balance.
1 tbls equals 13 mg calcium; 17 mg phosphorus; 51.6 mg magnesium; 585 mg potassium. Also high in B-complex vitamins, iron, chromium, and copper.

BRAN (unprocessed)

Has little food value, but adds the needed fiber, with 9 grams per half cup.

COD LIVER OIL

One-half of a teaspoon gives your dog 4000 units of vitamin A; 400 units of vitamin D; and 1.56 grams of unsaturated fat.

GARLIC

Garlic is high in potassium, and has vitamins B and C, as well as calcium and protein. In Europe garlic is a valuable medicine, helping to lower blood pressure; aid in sore throat and bronchial congestion. Also in a gelatin capsule.

KELP

More vitamins and minerals than any other food. High in A and B vitamins, and has 23 minerals. Makes a good additive to foods.

LIVER

Highest of all foods in iron; 70 times more copper than beef steak; in a half-cup, 7 mg iron; 44 mg copper; 5 mg zinc; One of best sources of chromium; high in potassium and selenium. Vitamins A, niacin and folicin also high. Desiccated liver tablets are versatile and nutritious.

OYSTERS (Eastern)

One-half cup has 56 mg calcium; 172 mg phosphorus; 67 mg magnesium; 284 mg potassium; 113 mg zinc; 8 mg iron; 241 mcg selenium; 12 mg vitamin C; 13 mcg folicin; 112 IU vitamin A.

SARDINES (Atlantic)

One-half cup equals 433 mg calcium; 556 mg `phosphorus; 44 mg magnesium; 440 mg potassium; 1.5 mg zinc.

YOGURT (Cultured)

One-half cup allows 208 mg calcium; 163 mg

phosphorus; 20 mg magnesium; 266 mg potassium; 1 mg zinc; plus others.

F O O D S *1/2 cup- in order of calcium-phos.-magnesium content.*

HIGH CALCIUM	milligrams
Dandelion Greens (cooked)	74- 22- 13
Yogurt (cultured)	208- 163- 20
Molasses (blackstrap)	1096- 272-412
Spinach	122- 50- 79
Black Beans	135- 420- 0

I.

HIGH PHOSPHORUS	milligrams
Sardines (Atlantic)	433- 556 - 44
Oysters (Eastern)	56- 172- 67
Liver (Beef)	12- 524- 26
Broccoli (Cooked)	47- 51- 19
Cabbage (Cooked)	25- 38- 11

HIGH MAGNESIUM	milligrams
Millet	3- 47- 38
Popcorn (plain, air-popped)	. 5- 11- 12
Banana	6- 20- 0
Avocado	10- 42- 45

HIGH POTASSIUM	milligrams
Black Beans	1,036
Banana	550
Sunflower Seeds, dried, hulled	667
Avocado	600

Shown below are some basic feeding menus, with the amounts of the Big 3 listed. The recipes can be made up in these amounts, refrigerated, and dished up to your companion in the appropriate servings, at the proper times. You will note that calcium and magnesium are added in powder form to the meals in order to keep the right ratios: Calcium/Phosphorus 1.2/1; and Calcium/Magnesium 2/1. These mineral powders can be purchased at your health food store.

RICE-TUNA-CABBAGE

	calcium	phos.	mag.
3 cups cooked Rice	33	360	105
3 1/2 oz. Tuna	20	306	0
5 1/2 t. Calcium	735	0	0
1/4 t. Magnesium	0	0	300
1 cup Cabbage	32	16	10
Totals	820	682	405

RICE-YOGURT-MOLASSES

3 cups cooked Rice	33	360	105
1 cup Yogurt	416	326	40
1/4 cup Molasses	548	136	206
1/8 t. Magnesium	0	0	130
Totals	987	822	481

MILLET-SARDINES-SPINACH

2 cups Cooked Millet	12	188	152
3 1/2 oz. Sardines	433	556	44
2 cups cooked Spinach	488	200	317
dash Magnesium powder	0	0	60
1/2 t. Calcium	220	0	0
Totals	1143	944	573

Use herbs along with your dog's meal. Supplement the enzymes. And use the dried cellular capsules as well. You'll soon see the contributions to wellness these therapies can make. You should know, however, just as with humans, not everyone is the same. What may work well for one may not do as well for the other. For example: Blue Flag may help with liver troubles for your dog, but not the neighbor's dog. Cornsilk may help to cure-up a prostate or urinary problem for one dog, but not another. Herbs do not come with guarantees. It's up to the caring guardian to work at wellness for the canine, just as you have done or are doing with your children.

You're probably already feeling good about being able to KEEP YOUR DOG WELL.........and knowing HOW TO GIVE YOUR COMPANION ADDED YEARS OF LIFE must give you a euphoric feeling as well.

Continue an optimal *balanced nutrition* for your dog. Learning his needs might take awhile before you see how each of the nutrients balance and effect each other, but it will all fall together eventually.

Supplement his diet with *vitamins, minerals, herbs, cell therapy and enzyme therapy*. Remember that his **vitamin and mineral supplements are useless if he does not have the enzymes** needed in his diet. So, be sure to see that your dog gets a quarter to a third of his total diet in uncooked foods. You can supplement with dry dog food, but don't rely on that as a complete diet for your dog.

See that your pet gets enough *exercise* to keep his weight in a good range, and his circulation optimal. Get out the ball and play with him. The value may be two-way.

Spend some time with your companion. Talk with him. A light massage does wonders for stress. You'll be pleased when you see what massage does for your pet. After a stressful situation for either you or your pet, you'll just *feel the stress draining out*. There is no substitute for *touch* while communicating. And *praise* your special canine whenever he deserves it too. You'll be amazed at the power of *praise*.

YOUR PET IS A

LUCKY DOG

FOR HAVING A

GUARDIAN LIKE

YOU